MW01612957

FATHERS
CRY, TOO

Other book by the author:

How to Plan a SPECTACULAR Family Reunion

Bill

March 7, 1998

I understand that you are as arrogant as my brother, an amazing thing! Please read this book with an open mind. Men who cried shared their pain so others can find comfort.

Jeanette Turner

FATHERS *CRY*, TOO
A Revelation of Hidden Tears

Geneva Turner, PhD, RN, CFLE

A Family Projects Book/CbGT
Columbus, Georgia

Published by:
Family Projects Publishers
P. O. Box 6427
Columbus, Georgia 31907

Cover drawing by Tres Dean Lansing, Michigan
Jacket design by Molley Nielsen, Columbus, Georgia
Library of Congress Catalogue number: 93-071885,
ISBN: 1-882977-07-6

Publisher's Cataloging in Publication
(Prepared by Quality Books Inc.)

Turner, Geneva.
    Fathers cry, too : a revelation of hidden tears / Geneva
Turner.

    p. cm.
    Includes bibliographical references and index.
    Preassigned LCCN: 93-71885
    ISBN: 1-882977-07-6

    1. Bereavement. 2. Fathers. 3. Infants--Death. 4. Father and
child. I. Title.

BF575.G7T87 1995   155.9'37
                         QBI95-20230

The Great Pretender

Oh yes, I am the great pretender,
Pretending that I am doing well
My need is such,
I pretend too much,
I am lonely, but no one can tell.

Platters

(From the group's number one hit song in 1956)

The efforts herein are dedicated to my husband, Ronney Revis, in memory of my father, George Robert Turner, and to fathers across the United States who shared their experiences with me. They allowed me to enter a most private region of their emotional being. Without their revelations, this book would not have been possible. For in truth, this work is a product of all the pain and suffering they have endured.

I extend a special salute to other fathers who read this book and *know*. In every locale and social strata, a father somewhere is in need of acknowledgment that he, too, suffers, in his unique way. These words were written for fathers who are young and old, rich and poor, incarcerated, free, and all others.

CAUTION

Before you ask the obvious, let me tell you that I am a woman writing about male grief! This book is not about the *ought to's* regarding fatherhood, nor is it about how men and women relate intimately. This book is a summary of thoughts, feelings, and needs shared by fathers who grieve.

DISCLAIMER

The names of characters portrayed in this writing have been changed to protect the privacy of fathers who participated in a study, and others who were, and are, clients. All fathers gave permission to the author to use their words to inform the public. Any similarities in name are merely coincidental.

Acknowledgments

Many people are acknowledged for their encouragement, understanding, and emotional support; and for their hospitality and assistance during the completion of the investigation that subsequently led to this book.

My brothers and sisters deserve special recognition for their contributions. Thanks to Alice T. Burch, Roland B. Turner, Milton Turner, Ricky Turner, Yvette T. Lackland, and Juanita P. Turner for their encouragement and timely deeds. My brother Melvin's support was nothing short of magnanimous. A special note of appreciation to my sister, Connie Turner, for making memorable sacrifices.

Other persons are to be thanked for their support and insight: Dr. Victoria Chinn Sang, VA Medical Center, Hampton, Virginia; Dr. Hattie Bessent, former director, ANA's Minority Fellows program, now residing in Florida, and W. Curtis Stephens of Hampton, Virginia.

I owe a debt of gratitude to the following people for their hospitality and for making significant contacts: Nancy

McGreevy of Birmingham, Alabama; Teresa McGreevy of Wilmington, Delaware; Sharon and Bennie Phifer of Cincinnati, Ohio; Joyce Sawyers Turner, Gary, Indiana; Alice Turner Burch, Radcliff, Kentucky.

Many support group facilitators, physicians, and nurses deserve recognition for realizing a need for my search. My sincerest thanks to the many eatery managers who checked to see if I was okay as I rested in their parking lots. Thanks to motel managers and security guards who somehow knew that I offered no threat, and to others who unknowingly allowed me to slumber in their parking lots.

My appreciation to truck drivers everywhere, who seemed to be my guardian angels as I drove thousands of miles while awake and asleep. One incident had a profound impact on my life.

After driving for what seemed to be an eternity, I had a few miles remaining before I reached the Texas border. Evidently, I fell asleep. I do not know how long I had slept. I remember being in the right lane driving a bit over the speed limit.

I was awakened by a voice that defies exact description, although it was soothing, booming, and raspy. *Wake up,* were the only words uttered by a voice that knew the protective cement curbing was about to end. I awoke immediately to find my car cradled between two 18-wheelers, and my tires and almost-new rims scraping the curb.

The cab of the truck behind me seemed illuminated by the bright lights he flashed to wake me. Both truckers honked their horns. My speedometer registered 87 miles per hour. Shaken and frightened, I waved one hand to let my rear protector know that I was awake.

I pulled over to the side of the road, said a prayer and regained my composure. I was just outside of Dallas. After a few minutes, I continued my journey home--slowly. The next day, my damaged tires and rims on the left side of my car were evidence of my ordeal.

I cannot end here without thanking several courageous souls who willingly read parts of this book and gave their comments: Connie Turner and Mercedes Gamez, Okinawa, Japan; Jim Pennington and Emma Johnson, Columbus, Georgia. To members of my dissertation committee at Texas Woman's University who allowed me one privilege--to study fathers using combined formats.

For these and other acts of kindness, to each person, I thank you!

Table of Contents

Preface

The experience of another is
not and never can be
evident to me, as it is not and
never can be an experience of mine
. . . we can see other people's behavior
but not their experience.
          R. D. Laing, 1967, *Politics of Experience*

S eeing is believing" is an adage that aptly describes
how society responds to a plea for help from anyone,
especially men. Designation of accurately placed
sympathy and empathy are based on identifiable cues and
clues. If cues of inner turmoil or joy are absent, a diagnosis
of need is not forthcoming, nor is a time for celebration set
aside. So it is with fathers.

Men are often taught to hide feelings that show loss of
control. They are also encouraged to deny any attributes that
connect them with femininity. So much of their emotional

life is denied, and even more of it is camouflaged. Emotions are confusing to most fathers and to men who choose to hide their feelings. It is no wonder fathers are wrongfully relegated to being towers of strength during adversity.

The information presented here is not intended to diminish the grief experienced by mothers when a baby dies. However, there are volumes of research and exposes published on the consequences of pregnancy, mechanisms of birth, multifaceted aspects of motherhood, and on how mothers grieve. These writings far surpass the minuscule number accumulated on any topic written about fathers and fatherhood.

"I must remain strong for my family." These words echo a distinct reality for most fathers during a crisis, and especially following the death of a baby. How long must this façade of strength last? When does a father deal with his feelings? In most cases, the answer is never. The situation then becomes more confused for everyone involved.

A major cause for concern is the inevitable eruption of repressed feelings that often lead to dissolution of relationships, marital conflict, and inevitable divorce. Are fathers supernatural towers of strength? Or are they real, feeling human beings who grieve in their special way? The mystery unfolds.

Prologue

How It All Began

As a child, after viewing television, I often wondered why other people's fathers were so unlike mine. They were either unbelievably sweet or unrealistically detached. In previous decades, and even today, newspapers seemed to sensationalize a lone, negative father who is made to portray millions of real fathers. But then, when I was a child I didn't know any fathers who fit the description I viewed on the television, and most in the media seemed farfetched.

I must admit though that I was as guilty as many

children. I thought that my father was the source of all money, could solve any problem, had x-ray vision, could foretell the future, never got tired, and could tolerate any kind of pain. You got it, Superman was alive and well in most households.

Millions of families have fathers who are active in their households. They are involved at every level of family life. Some fathers even shampoo their daughters' hair; others cook and sew. Participation in household chores is a way of life.

By the way, I preferred my father's shopping habits to my mother's. My mother purchased sensible items that worked and were practical, durable, yet stylish. She purchased groceries in much the same way. Practical and nourishing food was her mainstay. Dessert was prepared in moderation. Actually, she could have been a nutritionist.

"Pork is bad for you, don't eat too much," she often said. "You cannot think with such heaviness in your system. Stay away from fried foods . . . bad for your heart." She was a genius at baking cobblers, pies, and apple turnovers. Such goodness!

Dear old Dad was just the opposite. Although he was a stern, no-nonsense man, he was a kid's shopper. Lots of dessert! "Go and get ten of those cream pies" (nine kids and several shopping carts). "Okay, now you go and get me twelve ½-gallons of ice cream." Or was it ice milk? Whatever the case, it was sweet, and it was sheer music to my ears and to those of my sisters and brothers.

He also took us to shop for school clothes and special occasion clothes with similar zeal. I have a vivid recollection of one of those shopping trips. I was 11 years old, and on the program at church to read a paper. When it was my turn to give input on what I wanted, I announced that I wanted a pair of spiked heel shoes.

My father said in a startled voice, "You are too young, and you cannot walk in spiked heel shoes." I heard his words. I also knew that wisdom formed his response to my request. However, I just knew that I could walk in them if I had a chance.

I declared, in a moderate voice that was filled with respect for my father, "But that is what I want."

I got them! Beige spiked heels, so pretty and much too high for me.

Just before Easter, I put on my spiked heels as I had done days before so I could practice walking in them. I failed miserably, but I reassured myself that on Easter day everything would fall into place.

Easter night at church, my name was called. It took four years, it seemed, for me to walk - no wait - to stumble to the stage just a few feet from my seat. The crowd waited patiently for me to take my place. Of course, people snickered.

I finally made it to my place on stage, and I read my paper with as much enthusiasm as my bruised ego would allow. I welcomed the applause when I finished. I then gathered my energy for a long struggle to my seat, never to move again until the program was over. I remember wondering whether people around me could possibly hear my heart beating. To me, it pounded like Big Ben, but no one commented. My father walked over to me and raved about my performance. He never mentioned my wobble to the stage.

His glance to me was--lessons taught.
Mine to him--lessons learned.

Now, I can only imagine my father's explanation to my mother when he returned with us after shopping. At the time, I did not realize that the indirect lesson of my odd purchase would have such a profound bearing on how I communicate with men today. A more meaningful lesson for me was that communication is not always through the spoken word.

I learned as a child, long before nursing school, that evidence seen through behavior does not necessarily represent what a person actually feels. Also, feelings don't always come out of mouths in the exact way they are felt.

In general, most people, regardless of their behavior or verbal acumen, cannot hide what they show the world. A person's eyes will show you - that is, if you want to see what is really there.

Years later, and now as I reflect on my experiences in several neonatal intensive care nurseries, I realize that I applied my knowledge of fathers when introducing sick babies to frightened parents. I recall fathers as being almost comical during these introductions.

Even in an intensive care nursery, with all of its strange noises and equipment, fathers present a veneer that is seemingly of total familiarity. I knew better, and could see it in their eyes: a look of fear. Babies struggled for existence, and in time, parents became more comfortable with their delicate infants and with their surroundings.

Picture this: Two chairs placed near an isolette. Parents of a premature baby are in for a visit. Mrs. Patterson mentions that she will hold Alex. After about twenty minutes, I go over to where the Pattersons are seated.

"Mr. Patterson, don't you want to hold Alex?"

"Oh, I'll just wait until next time."

I knew there might not be a next time. I looked at him and saw that he wanted to hold his son so badly, but he was frightened. It was time to allay his fears tactfully, right now.

Alex was connected to a monitor, an IV pump, a temperature probe, and a continuous feeding pump. Maybe the most significant point is that Alex required assisted breathing with an oxygen source. He only weighed three and a half pounds.

With lightning speed, I switched Alex and placed him in Mr. Patterson's quivering arms before he knew what had happened.

I turned to Mr. Patterson and spoke closely to Alex's ear. "Alex, leave your father alone. Stop picking on him." Smiling, I said to Mr. Patterson, "You're going to be okay. Why don't you put your finger in his hand? He has quite a grip. Look at that fist."

A smile instantly replaced fear and uncertainty on Mr. Patterson's face.

His eyes seemed to express--I thank you so much!
My nod and glance to him responded--any time.

And so, since 1971, I have observed fathers and mothers as they interact with each other. Symptoms of conflict between couples often replace outward appearances of love and affection. Both conflict and divorces are common for parents whose babies are hospitalized because of illness or who eventually die.

As their babies struggle against insurmountable odds, why does this side of birth occur with death? Illness and inevitable death require positive energies of both parents. Fathers across the country offer insight. Please read their stories with an open mind.

This book is written to enlighten all readers. The message herein is that fathers grieve, as do all humans. Please understand that taking care of their family's needs is simply part of role performance for fathers; their behavior is not an indication of how any father actually feels.

The book is divided into seven parts:

Part I: Questions

Three chapters provide an overview of how the author arrived at the point of questioning fathers about their grief experiences. In asking questions about the grief of fathers, answers could not be avoided.

Part II: Insight

This section positions the topic of grief into reality for fathers and readers. The author shares strategies for approaching and learning about fathers. This section provides insight.

Part III: Experience

These chapters allow the reader a vicarious experience of pregnancy, delivery, and the death of a baby from a father's perspective.

Part IV: The Search

The search for answers includes descriptions of interviews with vivid excerpts from fathers.

Part V: Pieces

This section includes six topics that provide pieces of the puzzle regarding fathers grief and rationalizations for their behavior.

Part VI: Resolution

Practical information is included. Special admonitions for transgressors are included in a chapter titled, "Are You Guilty?"

Part VII: Appendices

Addresses for support groups, literature on grief, and information on an exciting newsletter: *Fathers Talk*.

PART I: Questions

He who asks questions cannot avoid the answers.

Cameroon Proverb

1

The Meeting - 1986

I could be anywhere right now, doing just about anything. But I am finally here in Illinois, a long way from Texas, my temporary home for the past year and a half. I might as well sit back and wait. For years I have speculated about fathers. At last I will finally have an answer.

It is a cool day for July, almost cold compared to the Texas sun. I feel absolutely lousy. Not my usual perky self. I am a nurse; I'm supposed to know better. To think, I was once considered physically fit! Now I feel stressed beyond belief after nothing but junk food, endless driving, sleeping in motel parking lots, rest stops, truck stops, and fast food parking lots. My newfound habits have caught up with me.

As I sit in my car at a small, old, rundown gas station on the outskirts of nowhere, I wait for a complete stranger to arrive. I reposition my can of mace and check my tape recorder in my briefcase. I am ready for just about anything.

Finally, I find a suitable parking space after shifting my position several times to get out of the way of oncoming cars. After several minutes, a car drives up and parks away from the gas tanks. A man I assume to be my anonymous informant gets out of his car and heads my way. A flash of dread comes over me. Maybe it's him and maybe it's not. As the man comes closer, I hear myself utter, *"It's him."* Just as his mother had described. Yes, he fit her description well. I had talked with his mother two days before. She said he would come, and he did.

For a brief moment, I hesitate. My supposed informant could be a robber or a serial killer. It was too late for me to be afraid now. I knew I would not drive off, nor would I pretend to be someone else if he were to ask. I needed his story. So I said my usual prayer and wondered what the heavenly Father thought of me.

My soon-to-be informant was over six feet tall, a muscular man with large hands that could wipe out my life in a matter of seconds. But as quickly as my terror appeared, it disappeared. The man walked with his head bowed, as though he was assigned to observe the ground. As he came closer, he lifted his face and looked toward my car. I saw a welcome sight.

He had the look of the others.

I knew I was okay.

He stopped a few feet from my car, asked my name, and told me to follow him. Again the fear returned, but only for a moment. I followed him in my car to our destination for the interview.

We drove a short distance to his apartment. At the time, it seemed as though it took an eternity. He once shared the apartment with Jane, the mother of his now-deceased daughters.

When we arrived at the apartment building, I was suddenly aware that this was a depressed area. The whole neighborhood was in need of repair. I parked my car and wondered if it would be in one piece when I returned, or whether it would still be there at all for my other interviews. *Well,* I thought, as I looked around to take in my surroundings, *that is what insurance is for*.

Jane met us outside. I extended my hand, introduced myself, and quickly established my purpose. She did not smile. She seemed upset.

Jane and Robert did not touch or walk near each other. I observed one cold glance between them. It seemed as though they were strangers. The tension between them, and her gaze through me, demanded that I quickly allay her fears regarding my presence.

Once inside, Jane sat on a huge, cushioned sofa on one side of the room. Robert sat on the edge of a chair near the door. I was directed to a comfortable chair in a corner of the room. To the dismay of my tired body, I acknowledged the comfort of the chair, only to fear falling asleep.

With introductions and explanations out of the way, I eased into the interview by asking Jane the first question. It was obvious she had no intention of leaving the room.

In a raspy voice that echoed my cold, I asked, "How did Robert respond when your babies died?" Jane seemed to brace herself before answering. She leaned forward, looked at Robert, then at me. In a shrill voice, she said, "He just didn't give a damn. He didn't cry at all. I wanted us to cry together." What followed seemed like an incredibly long silence.

The value of silence is something I had to learn and appreciate as a nurse. To get Jane's opinion, I would have waited forever. *Allow her to elaborate*, I cautioned my eager mind.

I had anticipated that her version of Robert's grief experience would be totally different from his. I wondered why she could not see what I saw. A man whipped by death. Dreams of joy and hope shattered by their unfamiliar replacement at a time when everyone should have had reason to congratulate him. Instead, he keeps a deep secret from his mate and the rest of his world.

His eyes were lost and hopeless, dark and distant. His

head bowed lower now than when he had met me at the service station. I knew his initial response would not really match his inner being.

After years of talking with fathers, Robert was no different. He was in control for now. Like the others, he chose to brush off what is real and play a game, hoping that I would not play one of pretend, too. But then, isn't that what a man is taught in American society?

2

One Father's Story

My interview with Robert took an unexpected turn when I posed the first question about his daughters. He shifted in his seat, stared at the floor, then left the room!

I really cannot describe how I felt at that point: amazed, shocked, horrified? Maybe a blend of emotions.

It's over, I thought initially. I have encountered problems in the past, but no one has ever walked out at the beginning of an interview. I looked at Jane and saw that her smirk had turned into a look of surprise. She bolted straight up and scooted to the edge of her seat.

We waited in silence.

Neither of us moved as we attempted to comprehend Robert's actions. I tried to distinguish the sounds that echoed from the adjoining room. Water was running. I heard dishes clang together in a container. Now it sounded as though he was placing them on a rack.

Why did he leave? Maybe this was going to be a revealing interview.

The noise from the neighborhood filled the room as Jane and I waited patiently, without even blinking. He will return, I tried to convince myself. I am not leaving.

Time passed.

Seconds, no, minutes.

How long?

I don't know.

I heard sounds. Again, the noise echoed throughout the room. I listened intently as Robert cleared his throat, again and again.

Silence.

Then he returned and sat in his chair as though he had never left. He leaned forward with his head down. I could see on his face that the words that followed were not easy for him.

"Well, see, I started drinking more, and a lot of times when I would leave there [the hospital] I would drink a lot. See, I'm not the kind of guy that . . . shows my feelings.

34

When I get sobered up it's still there, but I just keep it bottled up really, until something gets next to me. Then I just take it out in a physical way with somebody.

"Sometimes I try to start a fight . . . or drink something. I know that doesn't solve anything, that it's not a solution. But, uh, it helped me to get a little peace of mind."

If I could have predicted his reaction to my next question, I probably would not have asked it.

"Think back to the actual time of your daughters' death. How did you feel?"

Again, silence. I did not dare make a sound or a move. Jane and I seemed to have the same thought. She also sat frozen in position, waiting for his response.

Once again, Robert got up and left the room. Again, to the kitchen. I could hear him as he washed dishes. Running water and clanging dishes did not overshadow what he was trying to mask. I could hear him as he cleared his throat over and over.

At this time, I became aware of other sounds in the apartment. I could hear wind seeping in through a window. Uncertainty makes you listen.

Robert reappeared in the doorway and slowly took his seat. He responded to my question. "The only way I can describe it, uh, seriously, I felt so lonely, really . . . very hurt. I had to get away on my own and figure out some of the things that had happened. Things were getting out of control, and I have to be in control."

Robert is the youngest sibling in his family, yet he is viewed as a dependable protector for his older siblings.

"I have always taken care of my brothers and sisters. If I am not in control . . . no one is. If I show Jane a little weakness, the way it really hit me, she will believe that I am always going to be that way. So I ball my feelings up. If I am on my own, at home alone, then I can hurt, and cry and pray. I sometimes sit in my room and ask, why did it happen? I felt like someone picked me out of a crowd and beat the hell out of me."

As he continued to share his story, Robert seemed to forget that Jane was present and an avalanche of emotions exploded. "Something else she doesn't know about. I have been walking to the next city and back - some 21 miles away when the feelings get so bad. I have been doing it a lot. It helps me to think."

As Robert talked, Jane stared at him as though she had been made privy to a closely guarded secret. Earlier, she had told me that he must have a girlfriend. That is how she rationalized his hours away from home.

I discovered more than I could have ever imagined from Robert's story. In fact, so did Jane. She looked at this muscular and very pained man as though she was seeing him for the first time.

After the interview, Robert and Jane walked me to my car. This time their arms were around each other. Jane looked up at Robert. He looked away with a boyish shyness, knowing their lives would not be the same. Jane realized that her anger at him was unfounded. Who knows? Maybe Robert will move back home.

Once outside, I suddenly became aware of the activities in the community: people walking about and working in their yards. Was I paranoid, or were they were looking our way? Or were they glad for Robert and Jane, too? I looked around and finally grasped the culture of the neighborhood-one of concern. I was glad for my efforts.

I remember thinking that my interviews were turning out better than originally anticipated. Not only was I gathering information and learning more about fathers, but families were recovering as they revealed hidden emotions.

My car was still parked where I left it. I bid the couple farewell and momentarily focused on my next interview.

I looked back at Robert and Jane as I loaded my briefcase and tape recorder into my car. I smiled and thought, *It's going to be a good day*!

3

The Beginning--1971

1 971 was the year I realized that babies die. It was not a
new fact. The death of a baby, until now, had been
remote fiction I had read about in nursing school.

Every day during the fall of 1971, babies were admitted
to my new place of employment with illnesses that boggled
my imagination. I was fascinated by the activity in the
intensive care nursery when I was in school. Nurses who
worked there were virtually independent in their practice. All
of them had to be quick thinkers to survive. I knew that was
my kind of nursing.

Isolettes were everywhere. Monitors chimed and bleeped every second of every day. Respirators blocked walkways and stood against walls.

I was a newcomer to nursing, fresh out of school--less than six months. In those days, I could work sixteen hours or more in a row. Then I would go home at night still full of energy.

My first solo assignment was to a baby born prematurely to an older couple. Her name was Sara, "without an h," her father reminded us. Mrs. Jones had been pregnant three other times. Yet none of her babies had survived to the point of viability. In spite of Sara's serious problems, everybody was hopeful. This baby had to survive. The parents had endured so much.

The unspeakable finally happened. Around 1:00 A.M., when predictions of a slow night had been made by experienced nurses, and all monitors and respirators in the nursery seemed synchronized, Sara's equipment played to a different tune. Despite all attempts to save her short, precious life, Sara died.

That night, I learned more than I had ever imagined about the unbearable parts of nursing. Experienced nurses knew the events that were to follow concealed yet another aspect of nursing that would be difficult for a novice--talking with parents of a dead baby. No book ever written can describe what actually happens.

Through tears and uncertain actions, I readied Sara for her

parents' arrival. It seemed unfair now, to watch her lifeless body lie so still. She was perfect in every way except her heart and lungs were just not able to handle life.

While we waited, hugs flowed. We consoled each other. Our hopes for this family had ended once again.

Someone came over to me and whispered, "They are here." I watched as Sara's parents scrubbed their hands and put on gowns, as though they were still required to protect Sara as they had when she was alive. Another ritual that was completed without thinking.

Mr. Jones' arms seemed glued to his wife's body as he supported her. She cried in a soft whimper, her eyes swollen from weeks without sleep and tears too numerous to count.

They were escorted to a secluded spot. I carried Sara's still body in my arms, kneeled in front of them, and placed her in Mrs. Jones' arms. She loosened the blanket and touched every spot on Sara's body with her fingertips. Mrs. Jones' eyes shone with the pain of another dream almost realized.

I spoke words of comfort, hugged both parents, and noticed that Mr. Jones consoled his crying wife but gave no outward indication of his own involvement in Sara's life. This was a different man from the father who had visited every day and told us how Sara would not date until he gave the word and of how he planned to teach her about boys and making it in the world.

I looked into his eyes and saw the anguish that his mouth

could not utter and that his actions attempted to conceal. He whispered, "I'll take care of her" (meaning his wife).

Before I left, he said, "I'll come out to the desk in a few minutes if you need to see me about signing papers."

I repeated Mr. Jones words in my mind. *I'll take care of her*. Even then, as a novice, I wondered, *Who will take care of you?*

PART II: INSIGHT

A moment's insight is sometimes worth life's
experiences

Oliver Wendell Holmes
The Professor at the Breakfast Table

4

The Problem

I have been a nurse for more than twenty years, and I
have worked in almost every health care section of a
hospital. My observations of human behavior during
crises number in the thousands. Yet I am baffled by the long-
term effects surrounding the death of a baby. Perhaps the
most perplexing emotion parents have to overcome is the
psychological trauma precipitated by an elusive parenting
role. This overwhelming experience is shrouded by the
anguish many feel due to the overwhelming effects of grief.

When a baby dies, it is common to hear sentiments

expressed to the mother. Some people will even send their condolences to the mother via the father. It is common for these same people to avoid acknowledging the father's feelings. I often wonder why.

I interviewed a father who was approached by well-wishers after a funeral for his baby. I merely sat back and listened, offering very little verbal participation in the conversation as he described his painful story.

L. J.

"I think what really struck me was at the church when we had the ceremony. When we walked outside, all the people there walked over to Mae and started consoling her. I was standing there totally alone. I didn't feel jealous about it or anything, but it just *hit me.* I thought: Boy, this is really tough! I have strong feelings about this, too, but it is Mae who is getting the attention. I didn't feel angry, but it just hit me. It made me feel very alone, and like I just had to swallow my feelings and be the strong one. It was tough, it was really tough.

"I held back so much. It is hard to grieve, because I didn't know how. And I didn't get the support to do it, and in a way I didn't feel I should be grieving or letting it affect me. I had a really tough time, I am going to be honest, I was suicidal. I felt like a piece of myself had just been torn out and thrown down on the floor.

"Shortly after Roger's death, I had a near-fatal automobile accident. Long after that I went to the doctor because I had stomach pains and stuff, just always feeling down. I started exercising because my doctor told me I looked awful. In spite of all of this, I still became unglued."

Health problems like these experienced by L. J. are more common than you might imagine. Ninety-five percent of the fathers interviewed experienced some kind of physical illness. Most did not seek medical attention. Others admitted that some health problems have lasted for years. Still, this group of fathers has not sought medical intervention to eliminate or improve their problems.

Forty-two percent of the fathers interviewed remembered being in an accident or a near-accident. Forty-five percent of them said that they attended support groups, and 20% of this group did so unwillingly. Fifty-four percent of the remaining fathers considered support groups to be "pity parties." Some fathers in the study were emphatic that attending a support group was out of the question for them.

Only 30% of the fathers interviewed were perceived by their mates as needing support. Thirty-two percent of them considered their mate to be their closest friend, or someone with whom they could discuss their feelings openly.

The most frustrating problem for this group was escalating conflict. Improperly positioned frustration occurred at a time when the couple should have been bonding together for strength and support. According to fathers in the study who experienced marital problems, they separated without being able to discuss the real problem. Only a few fathers were unable to identify a reason for the separation.

5

Grief

As surely as we live, we will certainly die. Somewhere, and in some way, someone will miss us when we are dead and buried. The pain a person experiences is a measure of relationship intensity or grief. Grief is a phenomenon of complex emotions that carries deep mental suffering, distress, and deep sorrow.

A grieving person is usually sad, distraught, prone to tears, and left with a great sense of emptiness. People even experience grief with the death of a long-time pet, and others, to some degree, when an item of sentimental value is lost or temporarily misplaced. Even animals are known to grieve.

Delineated by Freud, the psychoanalytic term, hypercathexis is a process of mourning that requires the mourner to turn his back on the real world and invest free energy in the struggle to part with the loved object. In his writings, Freud suggested a more positive outcome for the bereaved person who faces up to the loss than the person who avoids thinking about it.

Confucius (Kunyfutzu) lived during 551 to 479 B.C. He is reported to have proposed a controversial, three-faceted theory of grief:

(1) grief should span a three-year period

(2) family members should gather about and support the grief-stricken

(3) in the case of death, funerals should be occasioned by nothing short of sheer lavishness. Of course, his philosophy was not without criticism.

Mo Tzu (480 to 390 B.C.), a renowned philosopher in his own right, took exception to Confucius' theory, finding only the second aspect acceptable. In spite of their differences, Confucius and Mo Tzu did agree on a more fundamental plane, according to H. Creel in *Chinese Thought From Confucius to Mao Tse-tung*. They agreed that the experience of grief is a normal response to the loss of a significant object or person. As a result, they suggested that family members and friends console the grievers.

For decades, stage theorists (Kubler-Ross, Parkes, Engel and many others) have attempted to explain the reactions of grieving persons by placing observed behaviors into overlapping categories (Appendix A). Yet much about the phenomenon remains enigmatic.

Most people are familiar with the stages. The first and most common stage for grievers is denial and shock. The grieving person, on hearing or discovering a loss, attempts to deny that a permanent detachment is imminent.

This stage can overlap anger. The grieving person is outraged about the loss or death.

Another widely recognized stage is bargaining. This stage includes appeal for support or desire to trade places, prized possessions, or habits to a higher power in return for the life of the significant person.

The final stage is acceptance or reorganization. In this stage, regardless of the terminology used to describe it, the grieving person starts to live again without the detached person in their life.

These stages of grief are classic for most people, especially women. However, role performance should be considered when the event of death dictates that someone take charge. As with all occurrences in life, a discussion on grief is futile without considering gender differences. One aim of the women's movement is to fight for changes in dealing with men. Mates and spouses remind their partners that equality exists.

Grief presents a different picture for men. In most situations, when a catastrophe such as death occurs, even health care professionals turn to the almost stoic male present and place a sense of duty on his shoulders.

Faced with keeping his family going, most men will postpone their grief. How is this possible? And why? When does a father deal with his own emotions? These are questions that require responses, especially when family dynamics is just that: interactions between the whole family.

Most fathers plunge into completing the details of a funeral and ensuring that postpartum care is in place for their mate. With his mind on such details, a father is able to avoid thinking about how he feels or what he needs at the time.

It is not surprising that fathers and mothers experience grief differently. Mothers get on with the business of grieving, the grief of fathers is often deferred to a less stressful time when performing their role as *caretaker* is no longer essential for continuity of the family.

Conflict and confusion arise when most mothers are ready to move on and fathers are just beginning to deal with the death of their child months and sometimes years later. However, postponed manifestations of grief either fester or erupt. In either case, the outcome is menacing and detrimental to healthy existence.

This imbalance in a couple's grief is not pathological. Both partners should express their feelings and acknowledge the other partner's uniqueness.

6

The Way It Is

Men and women are different. The world emphasizes this point the moment a baby is born. As soon as a newborn male is shown to his parents, wheels turn and motion is set to teach him about being a boy.

Pink is for girls, blue is for boys. And never the two shall meet. Okay, so little girls wear blue, white, green, ycllow, and a vast array of colors. In fact, baby girls can even wear red. But parents show very little variation in what baby boys wear.

At some point in our past, gender rules established approved behavior for boys and girls, and what is proper for each to wear. A few of those rules are discussed here.

RULE ONE
Frills in dress for girls, plain dress for boys. An important part of this rule is that boys do not wear pink.

Centuries ago, an anonymous person derived a rule that baby boys wear blue. Tradition has it, in this culture, that deviations from custom are sure to be precursors of homosexual behavior. Just an unspoken rule. Whoever is so bold as to go against the *no pink for boys* rule is certain to inherit stigma and crossed looks and words from relatives and friends. *They must want son John to become daughter Jane.*

RULE TWO
Big boys don't cry.

As soon as little boys learn to walk and utter a few sounds, they are taught the rule of suppression and repression. How absurd! Can you imagine falling down and nearly requiring the assistance of an orthopedic surgeon only to be told: *Big boys don't cry. You'll be okay. That didn't hurt, did it?"*

I have witnessed little boys who experienced an accident

at home or on the playground. From the look on their faces they deserve a good cry, a yell, or at least a whimper. Silence is what I observed, accompanied by a struggle to hold back tears. Is it no wonder that these same little boys grow up wondering when it is fitting to cry and still be in control as a man?

Little girls, however, are allowed every liberty imaginable in the emotion department. Watch a little girl merely bump her toe. Better yet, dress her in a frilly dress and put bows in her hair. Watch what happens when she sustains a minor injury. The entire family takes on the injury as though her toe had been amputated.

The injured girl then learns the feminine side of rule two. *It is acceptable for girls and women to cry.* So admonitions are given to little boys and support to girls.

RULE THREE

Men don't show emotions, nor do they get excited during any event other than sports.

With this rule, the stage is set for almost total closure to identification of emotions. Boys learn at a young age that it is unmanly to disclose emotions. Suppression of true feelings is often rewarded.

Initiation of these rules is obvious in the following scenario. It takes place in your average everyday household. A mother, a father and twins--a boy and a girl.

Jason was born at 9:00 P.M., and Joanie was delivered at 9:25 P.M. Now they are twelve months old, in a playpen while their mother, Carol, prepares dinner. Their father, John, enters the house after being at work all day.

Joanie is playing with her toy rattle. She is mouthing it, tasting it, really exploring her new, see-through toy. Jason is on the other side of the playpen beating his new rattler against the railing.

Hammering? Perhaps he is imitating observed behavior. At the moment, he is hitting an already frayed area on the safety latch.

Is there a difference in play behavior? If a difference exists, is it genetic or environmental? I do not know. Maybe a bit of both, but we do know that Dad just walked into the room and reinforced Jason's behavior.

"That's my boy." (big grin). "Hit it Jason."

He calls to Carol in the kitchen.

"Carol-l-l, come here and see this. Look at how strong Jason is."

He then walks over to Joanie.

In a modulated and very soothing voice he says, "Hi baby. What do you have there? Taste good?"

He leans over the playpen and tickles her.

Jason hits his hand with the rattler. Immediately he looks at his hand as though to acknowledge the pain. He then cries bloody murder. It hurts.

John tells him as he picks him up, "Hey, hey. It's okay my little man. It doesn't hurt. Let's not cry over that. It's going to be okay."

The stage is set in this family system for initial suppression of emotions for Jason. Throughout life, these gender differences are reinforced. In most instances, parental and societal influences attempt to ensure conformity.

Even nursery rhymes contribute to the *nice girl, bad boy* image.

What are little girls made of? Sugar and spice and everything nice.

And little boys? Cats, snails, and puppy dog tails.

With this riddle, and others like it, girls are taught to be emotional, pretty, and nice. On the other hand, boys are taught to be rough and tough and in control. This nursery rhyme may be the first introduction to gender differences that children receive from books. And so the differentiation is perpetuated further.

Role socialization for boys shapes their emotional future. In addition to suppressing emotions, males are supposed to seek achievement. They are to work toward getting ahead and not appear affected by unstable events.

Each gender identifies with sex-type appropriate behavior. From preschool age, children internalize attributes related to gender identity, first by observing their parents, then by noticing others.

This conversation occurred between preschoolers on a playground.

"That's not yours, that's for boys. You are a girl, you can't play with that," shouted James.

"Yes I can, too. Your names are not on it," screamed Ashley.

Martin seemed to ponder the whole issue and then spoke as though he was the final authority on the subject, "It's not for girls."

Not to be outdone, Ashley demanded, "Says who?"

"We do, that's who."

Once gender identity is discovered (colors, styles, behavior), appropriate behavior according to culture and societal punctuation is usually observed. Sex-typing is cemented as children begin to demonstrate the learned behavior and receive reinforcement from parents, other significant persons, and society.

Two schools of thought exist regarding sex role development and sex-typing:

(1) few sex differences in personality are evident that are not a function of learning,

(2) masculinity and femininity reflect norms and values that are internalized by children through direct cultural transmission.

According to D. Ullian, in Lloyd and Archer's book, *The Development of Conceptions of Masculinity and Femininity* in a chapter titled, "Exploring Sex Differences," a theoretical and ideological distinction are in effect.

Men suffer in many ways that may relate to the strain their emotional denial places upon their bodies. Compared with women, men die younger, have more heart attacks, and contract more stress-derived diseases.

Many authorities have acknowledged that men are less aware of their own emotional life, disclose themselves less to others, and find more difficulty in loving and being loved. Men have greater difficulty identifying and dealing with grief. In time, this will change, but for now, *that's just the way it is*.

7

Will The Real Father Please Stand Up?

U p in the sky."
  "It's a bird. No, it's a plane."
  "No, that's just my Dad. He's fixing the roof."
"You mean he's not Superman?"

My father could repair anything. Our house, gates, cars, the roof, dolls-even people. It wasn't until I was much older that I realized he was of average height for a man. Until then, I always envisioned him towering over me as he had when I was a child. He was known for finding a point for learning in any situation and even most objects.

I remember the anxiety I felt when I saw him at work. He worked for a railroad company and would walk across a moving train. To think, that same man had just helped me make doll clothes, with my designs, on my mother's sewing machine.

In the United States, a day is set aside to thank fathers for their contributions to child rearing. Father's Day has been celebrated in the United States for over 80 years. While listening to a sermon in 1909, Senora Smart Dodd got the idea of establishing a day for fathers after the speaker suggested a national Mother's Day observance. However, this special day was not proclaimed as an official national holiday until 1972.

The original intent was to designate a day for children to pay tribute to their fathers. Nonetheless, the holiday receives little fanfare except from merchants. Often, gifts given to fathers do not begin to compare to those given to mothers in the same families. Some of these gifts are accompanied by excuses .

Who are fathers, really? What do they know about their role? Actually, some of them know very little. In the not too distant past, and by middle-class standards, fathers were the sole breadwinners. In some families they were disciplinarians.

This last point brings to mind my own family life. My father's brown belt was called "Mr. Mind-changer." Most of the time, it simply hung in position as a reminder. I can hear him now. "So, you are having problems behaving? Let's see if Mr. Mind-changer can help you out."

That was in the days when a well-deserved spanking was not considered to be child abuse. James Dobson is a renowned authority on child-rearing. In some of his writings, he depicts fathers as caring and responsible parents who are baffled by some aspects of parenting, especially discipline.

In recent years, society has finally allowed men to grasp the total notion of parenting. But fathers have not always been as they are today--expected to participate in family life. By Anglo-Saxon standards, fathers during pioneer days, the Industrial Revolution, the Great Depression, and following World War II have progressed from the outer perimeter of family life to being central figures in today's society.

Fathers *have come a long way baby*, but certain experiences remain a mystery. If it were possible to ask a person from each historic time frame about the duties and experiences of fathers, each person would provide a dramatically different response. Yet each response would be quite descriptive for society's standards during their lifetime.

Years ago, a television celebrity regularly asked groups of precocious children questions about family life. On one memorable show, he asked the children about their fathers. Their responses were hilarious and quite poignant. He approached each child with a microphone as they sat in small chairs on a platform on stage.

"What does your father do?" he asked the first child.

"He makes money so I can have toys."

"What does he do at home?" He asked the same little girl.

"Nothing," she replied.

"Surely he does something."

The child looked up at him and said quickly, "He fixes things."

The celebrity moved to another child.

"Who makes decisions in your house?" He asked the next child.

Without hesitation, the child responded, "My mom says my dad *thinks* he does."

The studio audience roared with laughter. I suppose the viewing audience laughed as I did. At the time, I was too young to know why.

How does a man learn to be a father? The same way any other person in the world learns a role or occupation. Some learn by perfect example, while others learn by trial-and-error.

What is acceptable behavior for fathers? Who knows? New fathers without models for their role must work with logic and their hearts.

Expectant parents often attempt to imagine their

parenting roles the same way that actors might prepare for opening night of a highly regarded play. Then when delivery time finally arrives, just when both parents are getting comfortable with their anticipated roles, many "Opening nights" produce a baby who has to fight to stay alive. For some, the baby of their dreams is not forthcoming. Their opening night turns into an unexpected disaster.

Have you ever observed an expectant father in a toy store? What about a first-time father in a hospital waiting room, before or even after the delivery of his baby? One thing is certain: in both instances, 99.9% of the time you will observe a man who is exuberantly happy--nervous, but happy. Fortunately, you will find most fathers these days in the delivery room instead of waiting with other visitors - pacing and smoking cigarettes.

The father in the toy store will probably purchase more toys than he should for his unborn child. Fathers even describe to the last detail how often they and their unborn child will play with a specific toy.

The media is not viewed as a champion supporter of fatherhood. It is more sensational news to spotlight a story on a negligent father than it is to praise one who goes over and beyond the expected. So, young fathers without role models have a difficult time claiming positive father functions from the newspaper and television.

Nevertheless times are changing. As society becomes more flexible and home-oriented, roles for fathers expand to include more nontraditional responsibilities.

Real men don't eat quiche was a fad in North America in the '80s to emphasize a man's macho image of not eating food that seemed feminine. However, real fathers do it all. These fathers bathe babies, change diapers, style hair, and even cook in a kitchen without having the local fire department on alert.

If Margaret Meade were alive today, she would surely rephrase her statement that suggested the mood of fathering during her time: *Fathers are a biological necessity but a social accident.*

Margaret! Your statement smacks of inhumane thought. Who knows, maybe some problems encountered by fathers in their family role stem from insensitive comments and confusion that linger from statements published by well-intentioned authorities?

8

Roadblocks, Gatekeepers, and Other Unnecessary Stuff

D on't think for one minute that it was easy getting fathers to tell their stories. Think about the last in-dept conversation you had with a man. Who did most of the talking? Who revealed the most information, and who listened the most? A greater percentage of females are talkers and not active listeners.

But I encountered a different problem. In most agencies that deal with emotional aspects of life, women dominate the staff positions: in hospitals, support groups, Lamaze classes, physicians' offices and the like. Let's say they are coordinators or gatekeepers; they control access to most institutions and groups.

I found it extremely difficult when I approached most female gatekeepers regarding fathers and their grief. Everybody seemed to have an uninformed opinion regarding the ills of fatherhood. So I received a great deal of unwanted information from people who had absolutely no insight. Because they controlled access to fathers in their groups, unfortunately for me, and for those fathers, I was refused access. One gatekeeper said, "They won't talk to you, so why bother? Men just don't talk to anyone about those kinds of things."

I pleaded, "Allow me to discover this information for myself."

One person responded with an expected, "They will probably get angry, so I have to say no."

A great deal of time was consumed discovering my exact reason for proposing to study fathers. My need was simple: I wanted to gain insight from fathers in various domains to make the results more generalizable.

I soon realized that in our fast-paced society, people who interact with the public have carried the practice of interpreting other people's feelings too far. R. D. Laing (1967) explains my point: "I can see your behavior, but your experience is not and never can be an experience of mine."

In essence, people do not always feel the way they act. We should not assume that behavior is a true representation of the heart. Ask, if you do not know.

I encountered an infinite number of people who thought they had insight on male behavior, but who actually blocked progress in discovering fathers and their experiences. I was aided by some wives, mates, mothers, nurses, physicians, and most support group leaders; however, gatekeepers in institutions were a definite hindrance.

Now that the research is over, the number of times I was refused assistance seems almost comical. No father approached, directly or indirectly, declined to participate in the study once the intent was clear in his mind. What I received from fathers was a common response: a brief, characteristic stare, momentary lowered head, almost unnoticed softened voice, eyes that showed pain of revisiting a tragic event and then, consent to share their experience.

9

Lessons Learned

etting beyond gatekeepers was not my only problem in learning about the grief experience of fathers. My own prejudices, female socialization, and feminine interpretation of the world initially limited my entry into their experiences. But I changed all of that by observing men as they related to the world.

The study's format and other minor details were discovered quite by accident. For instance, it was late one evening, and as usual, I raced into a copy shop loaded with forms and a questionnaire. The place was crowded, and I was in a hurry.

When I could ease my way to the counter, I reached over several boxes for a stationery color chart. Instantly, I selected peach, maze, lavender, and pink. I didn't give much thought to my choices, but later I realized that my selections were considered feminine by most men.

At that moment, the attendant said, "May I help you?" I froze, as though I was suddenly graced with insight. I looked around the room and became aware of all the men present. I then concluded that a simple stationery selection could have feminine and masculine consequences.

I turned to the men in the copy shop and queried their preference. I asked, "If you receive several letters, and the envelopes are these colors, which one would you be more inclined to open?"

My request for clarity was met with a flurry of unsuspected responses. Most of the men laughed. It seemed as though they shared an inside joke.

A tall man with weather-beaten skin was the first to speak up. "You got the wrong colors lady."

"None of them ma'am," yelled a voice I could not locate in the crowd.

"I like blue myself," was the response from a man in blue overalls and a blue striped shirt.

"What else you got?"

I flipped the color chart to hues of blue and gray and pointed. "What about these?"

"Now, any of those are okay. They are more for men."

I could not begin to count the heads that nodded approval. I selected blue stationery with gray envelopes. How simple and yet how profound. I realized that each step in my study would have to consider masculine choices.

Another lesson learned, quite by accident, was very frustrating for me at the time. I interviewed a father at his office. The building was massive, and his company was huge. The security check to enter the facility was frightening.

When he entered the room, instantly, his eyes told of inner turmoil and pain. He validated my impression of his experience during the interview.

My agenda included conducting an interview according to a published guide.

It didn't work.

As soon as our chairs were placed and he agreed to have our conversation recorded, he began his story.

I was overwhelmed by his freedom of expression. He talked about his experience and required no prompting. It would have been totally inappropriate to pull out a structured interview guide at that time. How would I have responded? What could I have said? "Wait just a minute, we must conform your responses to the questions on this totally inappropriate guide." Besides, the information he shared was rich with insightful experiences.

My informant talked nonstop for two hours. My part of

the conversation with him, at that time, consisted of "yes, uh-huh, right, okay, I see, and, an then." Later, when reading a transcript I counted at least 100 times that I said "uh-huh" alone. He cried, cursed, beat the table, and best of all for me, he was the first of several informants to redirect my study to its final form.

I actually learned several lessons, but this one was quite amusing. I should have anticipated the outcome. Again, while exploring options for retrieving information from fathers, I carried out part two of the study. I mailed scenarios to fathers with self-addressed and stamped envelopes. I also enclosed a copy of BEM's Sex-Role Inventory.

This inventory is important in research because of its succinct responses and ease of completion. In 1976, Sandra Bem designed a method of determining sex-role identification by listing 60 personality characteristics that are rated on a scale of one to seven. The number one on the scale is never or almost never true and seven is always or almost always true.

There are four sex-role categories when scoring personality characteristics using BEM's Sex-Role Inventory: masculine, feminine, androgynous, and undifferentiated. The four sex-types derive definition from characteristics internalized from societal, individual, and shared expectations. The masculine sex-type comprises characteristics expected of males; feminine sex-types score high on characteristics assigned to females. Androgynous individuals score equally high on masculine and feminine characteristics. The undifferentiated sex-role is just the opposite of androgyny; this person scores equally low on female and male characteristics.

Almost all of the mailed scenarios and inventories were returned. The scenarios were neatly answered and each inventory returned classified the men as feminine. I called one of the participants and asked if he had completed the information I mailed. He confirmed my suspicion. He said, "No, I didn't, I asked Joyce to fill it out for me. She knows me. I don't like filling out anything like that. Men don't like that kind of thing."

Back to the drawing board. I knew then that the other fathers had probably done the same thing. This method of data collection was eliminated.

When I revised the study for the third time, I considered all the lessons I had learned. I also evaluated the insight provided by the men in the copy shop and others. My new approach was simple. I would learn from fathers about their experiences of grief after I learned more about the behavior of men and fathers.

My serendipitous discovery of the *right fit* in research methods is actually decades old. It is used quite extensively in Europe. It is called ethnography. Ethnography offered an opportunity for me to discover fathers' grief through grounded theory--information that comes from informants.

Bronislaw Malinowski wrote that the goal of

ethnography is to grasp the native's point of view, his relation to life, and to realize his vision of his world. Instead of studying people, ethnography means learning from people.

James Spradley is also an authority on ethnography. He wrote that ethnography offers the chance to step outside one's cultural background and comprehend the world from the viewpoint of other human beings.

The study was based on principles of ethnography that all focus on learning from the people studied. Therefore, the information presented here is a result of that approach to studying fathers' grief and many lessons learned.

PART III:
EXPERIENCE

Let him speak who has seen with his eyes.

Zaire Proverb

10

Duty as Usual

The Hillermons' first baby has been dead less than one hour. They had been married for ten years and had accepted their childless fate until Sage discovered that she was pregnant. Finally, fertility drugs had worked. Everything was going great with the pregnancy. Long months had passed. They thought that this time they would deliver a full-term baby.

Three weeks before her due date, Sage felt stabbing pain in her lower back. Then a great gush of bright red blood filled her panties and spilled onto the floor.

This is not supposed to happen! Mike shouted inside his head as he tried to reassure Sage. She was hysterical. He tried to appear calm, but it was a losing battle. They both had wanted this baby so badly. Their baby had become part of every conversation and their lives long before Sage wore maternity clothes.

"Sage, I have decided," Mike announced to his wife one day, "Jamie is going to attend that new day care center near Forest Hills. I almost forgot to tell you, your brother Joe came by while you were out with his wild kids. What does he feed them? Jumping beans? I don't know about Jamie playing with those kids. Maybe when she is older."

Sage smiled and twirled her fingers in the air to suggest how hopelessly happy her husband was when he announced yet another new idea for Jamie's unborn life.

"Now, Mike," Sage said, "Joe is just a big kid himself. He is so close to his children."

Sage rubbed her stomach with both hands, as though the baby could feel her and hear them. She remembers how she felt when her brother and his wife, Ellen, came to visit. It seemed that Joe could not keep his hands off of Ellen's protruding abdomen. Now Mike was the same way, and she loved every minute of it.

"Do you hear your overprotective father, Jamie?" Sage rubbed her stomach as though the gentleness would help

Jamie respond.

Mike paused for a minute, looked at Sage and said, That's how I am going to be with Jamie. I'll enjoy every minute with her."

Sage replied, "Now yesterday you were on a kick about Jamie looking like you, with big feet like my side of the family. What's next?"

But those long-ago ideas will not happen now. Mike's thoughts are interrupted by a nurse as he sits waiting for Sage's doctor to appear.

"Mr. Hillermon, you need to sign some papers and then go to the third floor. Get the elevator, take a left, then two doors down the hall is Ms. Gibb's office. She needs to talk with you about an autopsy."

"Where do I go?"

"I'll show you later. While you are here, have you decided on a funeral home?"

"No, no, I--I, don't have any idea. When do you need to know?"

"Well, right now, because the morgue will need that information."

"I'll call my mother-in-law. She will have a name for me." Mr. Hillermon goes to a telephone, and calls his mother-in-law.

"Hello Mom, it's me again. The hospital needs to know

what mortuary to call for Jamie. Which one should we use?"

"Here is the number dear: 800-7878."

He barely heard the trail of numbers. He knew she would blurt the telephone number out as though she had heard the nurse ask him for it. She was always on top of everything.

"How is Sage? You take good care of her now. You know she has to be hurt, just almost out of her mind. This baby meant so much to her. I was almost out of the door when you called. I'll be there in 20 minutes."

Mike Hillermon has heard the unimaginable from everyone. Now his mother-in-law has reinforced it. He begins the long process of putting his grief on hold as expected, while he attends to details of the immediate situation.

11

Camouflage

As he walks slowly to do as he has been told, Mr. Hillermon has to wonder, if anyone has noticed that he is also hurt and distraught by Jamie's death. After all, he and Sage are both Jamie's parents.

Everything in their lives has changed in a matter of two hours. It seems as if they had just finished a conversation about the kind of paint for Jamie's room and the colors Sage would use to decorate the odd-shaped space that faced the front of their new home. A new home they had dreamed about when they started their family. But now, their family is back to two instead of being three.

For months, Mr. Hillermon had talked to Sage's stomach. Jamie had responded. He had called Sage's protruding abdomen "big tub," and Jamie was playfully named "Bumble bee" because of her movement all over the place when he put his mouth on Sage's stomach.

Here, there, and everywhere Jamie had raced and punched and kicked poor Sage. In her way, she let her Dad know that she recognized his booming voice. He had loved it when he was awakened during the night with a quick kick to the back, as if Jamie was making sure he had not forgotten her.

"Hey, wake up over there, she seemed to say."

He and Sage would laugh and talk about breast-feeding and babysitters. But he had thought about much more. College and marriage had filled his thoughts long before he knew the baby was going to be a girl.

If we have a girl, she will not date until I actually meet the boy's parents. I will have to know all about him. She will be at least 20, maybe 18 if she is good.

My son will own a car and have plenty of girls calling him every day, well, maybe not so many. But he will play football, basketball, baseball, or something. He'll be like me.

But now, their dreams were not turning out as they had anticipated. He keeps thinking over and over, *Babies are not supposed to get so close to life and then die.*

He walks down the corridor as though in a trance. He is

made aware of his surroundings by the countless corridor lights overhead that guide his path.

"Ms. Hudson, here is the number for the mortuary. Will you give me directions to those other places? You said I needed to sign papers?"

Off he goes, dry-eyed, seemingly confident in attending to the needs of his wife and arranging the burial of his baby. To an outsider viewing his behavior, he is detached from the situation, almost devoid of feelings for the baby. What people see is performance of duty. What they do not see is a distraught man who begins to feel put upon because no one acknowledges his feelings.

He doesn't want pity, nor does he want a long conversation. All he wants is for someone to say, "I know you are hurting, too."

That's all.

But no one does.

Instead, he is given more chores, more duties, more tasks to perform by everyone who comes in contact with him. The camouflage was never intentional. In fact, he just did not know what else to do.

PART IV:
THE SEARCH

Truth is on the march, nothing can stop it now.

Emile Zola, J'accuse

12

Sharing

I have vivid memories of each father's story as though the interviews occurred only yesterday. In reliving them, in addition to the excitement of gaining entry (completing a revealing interview with a father whose story provides insight), I recall barriers, coincidences, and close encounters that were both laudable and disastrous at the 11th hour.

Fathers did not appear out of the blue in the beginning. My efforts to enhance the study required advertising, word-of-mouth recommendations, meetings with support group leaders, enthusiastic and convincing conversations with physicians and nurses, vigorous appeals to spouses, other relatives, friends of fathers, and fathers.

Some of my techniques worked and some did not. However, any time I presented my story to a father, on each occasion, I gained entry.

After driving for endless miles, I finally yielded to my need for sleep. I did exactly what I had always been cautioned not to do: I pulled into a rest stop at 2:00 in the morning. Money for a hotel was out of the question, and by that time all the commonly known eateries were closed. I found a spot, positioned my mace, created a bed out of my small car seat, and behold, I saw safety nearby.

I heard people speaking Spanish. I saw a young man place a lawn chair on the cement walkway just above the steps close to their van. Two teenagers gingerly and very methodically helped an elderly woman to her place in the chair.

I immediately cranked my car and switched parking spaces as fast as I could--next to them. It seemed that with the care and love they showed the elderly woman, I would be safe for a much-needed rest.

I was awakened a couple of hours later. Someone had bumped my car. I felt as though I had slept for hours but it was only 3:30 A.M. The family was leaving. I recorded over eight thousand miles as I drove from city-to-city. I judged my safety with people I interviewed similarly to the way I assessed this family.

Driving was not always a task, as it may seem. It provided opportunities for introspection between interviews. I had time to dress up in restrooms of local eateries and hotels. I did not want to hinder my time with fathers by invading their domain even further by venturing into another part of their home. I was a guest and not an inspector.

Interviews were conducted in offices, lobbies, homes, restaurants, university conference rooms, parks, my office, various locations in hospitals, over telephones, and following support group meetings. Locations for interviews were selected by fathers. I agreed to any place that seemed safe.

Grief experiences included in this chapter are excerpts from in-dept interviews with fathers who were African-American, Caucasian, and Hispanic. Their ages ranged from 24 to 41, with an average age of 33.24 years. Most fathers were 28 to 32 years old.

Some fathers had incomes of six digits or more per year, while for others that figure was not imaginable. Some homes visited contrasted with their occupants emotional moods by their palatial-like beauty, while others gave evidence of the depression that dwelled within.

Only a few excerpts are included from the massive stories accumulated over the years. Each father tells his story in his own unique way. Prompts were used to ensure that similar information was obtained from each father.

Fathers cried and hit furniture, their fists, or other parts of their bodies. Some fathers were very tense, their hands gripping the arms of their chairs so firmly that the blood seemed to drain from their knuckles.

Changes in voice quality at certain points were very noticeable. Some fathers whispered and even changed the subject when their mates entered the room. Others laughed nervously throughout their interview.

I recall that a few interviews were close calls. There were occasions when I thought: *An argument is going to occur any second now, and I am in the middle.* I wanted to tell some fathers to keep their voices down. Especially when it appeared that problems existed before I arrived at their homes.

Some interviews were canceled at the last minute. Actually, two telephone interviews were unforgettable and ended with heated altercations that I could hear before our conversations ended.

I was amazed on many occasions by the similarities of the fathers' words and personality types despite the geographic and cultural separateness. Fathers who knew absolutely nothing about each other, who were different in every way, expressed their turmoil almost verbatim.

The excerpts that follow are unedited. They are included to inform the reader and to provide words of wisdom from fathers in their own way.

Carson

Carson began talking almost as soon as he walked into the room. He sat down, placed a notebook on the table and gave me permission to record the interview. He relived his experience from that point on as though I was not present.

"I felt extremely cheated by everyone. Brent's mother was never there. I went in to see him every day. I was always there. When she came, they set up one chair for her to hold Brent while he died instead of me. I will never forget that; I will never forget it. (He pounded the table with his fist.)

"They were okay to me at first. The visiting times were supposed to be twenty minutes every two hours, and there were times they let me stay longer. I felt I was related to the hospital personnel, I was there so much. But all of that changed the day she came to visit.

"I had custody of Brent since birth. He was mine. I had to worm my way in to hold him. Didn't they read the fucking chart? (Carson stood as he talked. His body weaved and swayed like a worm as he got closer and closer to the floor, mimicking how he felt when the nurses placed one chair by Brent's isolette.).

"I didn't protest, you know, I just kind of shut out the anger I was feeling. Even though we were having problems, I thought I had to be strong for her. She didn't want the marriage, and Brent seemed to be far from her mind. But people automatically gave her all the sympathy, and not me, never me. They just assumed that she must hurt more since she is the mother. She went on about her life after he was born, a life without Brent.

"I thought, did I screw up? It is difficult to survive. I need to be held, I still need it and it still helps. I keep a diary. I try to write in it every day. *He pushed the notebook toward me.* Sometimes the memories get too much and I can't write."

Carson leaned back in his chair, his hands to his face, and cried.

Henry

Henry was very expressive and animated as he shared his story.

"I was so angry at the way they handled Ragin, like she was nothing. I told them so. I had to protect her. There was this invisible entity around Ragin that I could not battle, I couldn't get hold of it to really battle it.

"So that ate me up a great deal. That really built up in me to the point that after three or four months, after she died, and I had gotten my wife through the initial period of depression and crying. One day I just felt like crashing. I thought, 'Why am I going through this sudden emotional outburst this far down the line?'

"When Ragin died, I just knew that I couldn't let this happen again. If Jane came up pregnant, I don't know what I would do. I just don't know what I would do. I felt like I was floating around in void.

"See I'm a big guy and people automatically think I can handle everything and that I don't need help. But I need help with this.

"I just needed to get away. I haven't taken a vacation from school or work in so long. I went through all of that and didn't take off but a week. I still attended class.

"I want to get away for awhile. There is nothing I want to do--just sit on the beach."

Dane

I felt very comfortable in Dane's home. He did not have difficulty recounting his experience.

"This is the first problem I have ever come up against that I couldn't throw on more manpower, or more money, or more effort to have it fixed. That is the first time that has ever happened to me in anything you know.

"I thought, 'It's my fault, I did something wrong, there was something wrong with me genetically.' The other thing that I felt was in spite of all the people around me, because I was apart from Helen, I felt totally alone. I felt like I would be alone the rest of my life.

"When the thoughts would start hurting too bad I would pick up a project or something I knew I could do well, something that I could control and that was the key. I did more for my company in that period. I was like a superman. The adrenalin was just pumping, because I couldn't cure Billy. The only way I could make myself feel good was to do things I knew I could do.

"People would come up to Helen and ask, "How are you doing, how do you feel, can I help you?" They would come up to me and say, "How is Helen?" As though to say, you are okay, we want to know about Helen. I wasn't jealous of the concern for Helen, I was equally concerned about her. But it really would have been nice to know if somebody was pulling for me, too.

"The worst thing anybody can say is: "I know just how you feel." I got a lot of respect for somebody who says, "I understand that you are in a lot of pain right now. I can't understand your feelings totally, I have never felt them, but I know somebody I can ask to talk to you."

"It is the toughest thing in the world for a father to get in a funeral procession going away from the hospital with his wife still in the hospital. The next is knowing that your child's life does not exist."

Jay

Jay's wife was pregnant. She met me at the door and left immediately to go shopping. She returned at the conclusion of the interview. At the door before leaving, she whispered, "I hope you can get him to talk, he has a lot inside that he has not dealt with."

Jay discussed Kerry's life and death and said that it was his role to be concerned about his wife. He also said he understood why people did not ask about him or try to talk to him. In essence, everything was fine. Yet, his hands were clasped so tightly that his knuckles were white, his eyes were red, his voice tone changed, and his color was flushed.

His verbal response inclined toward curtness, as he answered with "yeas" and "okays." He maintained this demeanor throughout the interview despite attempts to get him to verbalize the pain his physical appearance did indeed suggest.

At the conclusion of the interview, he led me through his home toward the front door. Jay's interview was the first I had conducted, at the time, where it was so obvious that his words were not congruent with his nonverbal cues. Not to be outdone, I decided that the conversation could not end in that manner. I noticed his flower arrangements and commented on the unique and assorted arrays.

Without acknowledging my compliment, he said, "I don't

know anything about you and you don't know anything about me. I just can't open up to you."

I said, "But your eyes have told your story for you. Your mouth doesn't have to say anything. Your body has done it for you."

He added, "So you know, huh."

Part of the following interview is a result of what Jay shared with me from that point.

"In the intensive care nursery, all the blinds were kind of closed, except for one had this little opening so I could see through it. It was such a scary thing to me. I could see all the nurses huddled around him.

"I couldn't see him through all the doctors and nurses. I was out there in the hall by myself and didn't know what was going on. I was trying to calm down but panic started to set in. I thought about my hopes and dreams for Kerry. I kept feeling out of it. I kept trying to take control of myself."

Doug

Doug's wife was present. She sat slumped in a chair next to him with tears in her eyes. Prior to the interview she stated that her husband had not expressed his emotions to her.

"Granted, I did not carry those babies nine months, but for nine months I knew they were there. I would feel her stomach when it moved. I could feel the babies, and I watched them be born. I was there the whole time, and I cared for them just as much as she did.

"Yes, I wanted someone to care for me, too. That would have been great, but that wasn't how it's supposed to be. You're supposed to be the strong one. It hurt. I would walk off into another room and wipe the tears away. It was hard.

"I felt like hitting someone. I needed to release some of this, to just sit and write out what I was feeling.

"One day, my brother and I went shopping at a local discount store. We went to the stereo equipment section and this man had two boys with him. The man touched and turned knobs and pushed buttons. One of the boys, about eight years old, reached up and turned a knob. Instantly, the man backhanded him. He knocked the little boy behind a box.

"I hit the man across the chest and asked him, 'What are you doing? Come on and mess with me. Don't hit that boy

again. You can't do this to a child because you'll lose them.'
I am not a violent guy. It's just that since Ricky's death, I
have felt like hitting someone or something. I wonder when
will the hurt go away?"

Phil

From the beginning of the interview, I knew that Phil still harbored not only grief, but anger. Someone had treated him unfairly during his experience.

"I felt frustrated as a parent. I shut off my feelings. I couldn't do what I wanted to. When Erica died, it was like half the mafia was there because we felt that we had to be involved. But we could not. She was in the ICU. We had many clashes with her doctor. I was angry most of the time. Later, another doctor was assigned. He seemed to understand what was going on with us. He would inform me of what was going on.

"The hardest thing for me then was trying to get my mother to understand how I felt when Erica died. She thought I should be able to deal with it quicker and better. It just tears you apart.

"I've got to admit, I get very involved in my work. It is one of my best escapes. When you have waited 30, 40, 120 days with a baby in the hospital, not knowing what is going to happen next, let me tell you, that will break you unless you have a very solid foundation. It will break a marriage.

"If I see a movie about a parent and their child, it will bring memories of times when I had hope for Erica's life. It would have been nice if things had turned out a different way, but that did not happen. It is easy for me to accept what happened. All I have to worry about now is what I can control. I worry what we are going to do with our lives? I often wonder about what I actually have physical control of."

Thomas

Thomas did not require prompting to share his story. He introduced all of the pertinent topics discussed by other fathers.

"When the nurses were saying they couldn't find the heart beat, I wanted to believe that it was because Lori was screaming so loud. She kept saying, "What's wrong, what's wrong with my baby?"

"I asked them, do you hear anything yet? I wanted to believe that she was so loud that is why they could not hear. So I put up a front for Lori so she wouldn't get more hysterical, but I knew something was wrong.

"One thing we're finding now is that a lot of people are asking, "What's the matter? It's been five months, you should be over this by now." I just respond to them; sometimes I'll say yeah, I know. It's just obvious they have never had a child die. I knew everyone would ask, "Why? What happened? When is the funeral?" I kept thinking how I didn't want to deal with that.

"Sad and sorry are not strong enough words, but I--I don't know a word to describe it. It hurt a lot. I cried inside and just couldn't in front of my wife.

"The cemetery is close to where I work, when I need to be alone, I go by and let my feelings out. Sometimes I stay a minute or so and sometimes I stay much longer."

Joe

Joe laughed nervously throughout the interview. Initially, I thought the noise in the hospital lobby would distract him as he recounted his story. However, as he described his experience, he seemed totally oblivious to the activity and sounds.

"You know, I didn't want to be home. I guess I didn't want to deal with it. It was hard enough for me dealing with my feelings, let alone to come back home and see her that way. I thought, 'Oh, you're a bastard for thinking that way.' Maybe that's that macho image coming out. Somebody has to be strong in times like these. Well, I have to be the one to show people that I can continue.

"Yet I felt so alone going through this. Jennifer couldn't help me, and I think that was the hard part of it. I had no one I could turn to. At least she had me to turn to. But we had to go on with our lives.

"Friends were supportive maybe the first couple of weeks and after that really nothing has been said about it. Everybody has to experience grief in their own way. As a matter of fact, Jennifer and I talked about that. The way I experienced it was a lot different from the way she did. She was more open about it than I was. I think that was it. She was more open about her feelings. You could see it more with her than you could with me.

"I didn't go to my priest for advice. I really didn't turn to anybody. I just sort of said to myself, 'Okay now Joe, what are you going to do? How are you going to deal with this?' I really didn't have anyone to talk to. I don't know, I felt like it was my own problem. It was my own grief.

"I haven't talked this much to anybody about my feelings. I wanted to hit someone bad. I was so angry, and at the same time, I wanted to cry and hug Jennifer."

Jack

Jack's wife, Grace, was present for part of the interview. She said, "He still has this macho thing that he is supposed to fix everything. He has failed if he doesn't and that is just not true."

Jack had visitors when I arrived, so the interview was delayed. The delay was worth the insight Grace provided about Jack. During the interview, he shared his experience as though it occurred yesterday.

"One bad thing about this. It doesn't matter who I am with or where I am, I can usually do something, especially for Grace. I take care of things for her like when her grandfather died. I could handle things one way or another. I couldn't do anything about my child's death.

"With my kids by my first marriage, if they ask me for something, then I will deal with it. I guess the biggest problem I had was that there was nothing I could do. It sort of belittled me that I could not solve this problem.

"I didn't hold Taylor. I think I was afraid, but I kept wanting to. Now I wish I had. I was sad and hurt inside. We still have his room set up. I go in there sometime.

"All I needed was for someone to say, 'How are you doing, or do you need to go out and get a beer? Or do you need to go for a drive?' I didn't get that. I used to drink a lot, but now I can face facts."

Floyd

Floyd's wife, Mary, was present during segments of the interview. Her memory of Floyd's experience was totally different from his recollection of events. She constantly attempted to discount his story. Floyd required few prompts. In spite of interruptions from his wife, he offered his story easily.

"My priorities have totally changed. I used to be like everyone else--a dream of a beautiful house, cars, pool and so on, all the materialistic things. Now the only thing I am concerned about is being happy. I still have my ambitions, and I still want to be successful, but I don't put that much emphasis on anything. I had not cried in years and years. And now you can read that men need to cry because it is good and that it helps to release frustrations.

"When Jill was born, I broke down and cried like a baby. I mean, I wanted a girl so bad. And at some point in my mind I started to think, 'Well, God is taking her away from me. Maybe I haven't been leading my life right.'

"I think about Jill each and every day, especially when I see a baby. Then I'd go out to the cemetery, and I would force myself to just break loose or whatever you want to call it, just sit and cry, and release the pressure. The most painful thing for me was losing my daughter. Then I felt really bad because I felt that her mother was just excluding me from the whole deal. She acted like she was the only one who felt the pain. I needed Mary to realize that I needed her."

Ross

Ross stared at the floor in his office and spoke softly as he offered his experience. He shared his memory of Lynn being transferred to an intensive care nursery at another hospital. He later informed his wife, Blair, of Lynn's status.

"I was playing politics. I said maybe she is okay because she was so beautiful on the outside. When I got back to the hospital, they started putting all this other stuff on me. I--I just couldn't believe it. Then I had to face going back to the hospital to tell Blair.

"I knew I had to snap out of it because I had to be the stronger one. I was out of control. I felt like I had been ripped apart, like someone had kicked me. I was so beaten down. I wanted to get away and think about all of this.

"I wondered how I would handle the whole thing. I thought about God. I felt so isolated and confused. I needed someone to talk to. I even thought about starting a group. I needed to be hugged, and I wanted to talk with Blair."

Edward

We discussed common interests. Edward's wife, Paula, was present. They seemed uneasy about the interview at first. Later, their uneasiness vanished as their conversation flowed. Their twins had been dead a short time.

"I told the physician that God would save our twins lives. She said, "Well, so far in medical history, God has not determined to save the life of a 23-week-old baby." She walked out of the room. It was very difficult for me to deal with her. She was so insensitive.

"I was offended by what she said. But that was the least of my worries at the time. I thought what she said was inappropriate. The twins were later found to be 27 weeks. They had a good chance of surviving.

"Paula and I are best friends so we can rely on each other. What we needed at the time was a more understanding physician. That doctor was replaced immediately. He was much more understanding. He even asked my opinion on matters as though I knew what to say. I liked that. At least, don't forget that I am present.

"I thought mostly about how I was going to help Paula. I was so distraught. I just needed for someone to say that everything was going to be okay."

William

Attempts were made to interview William in person. However, because of his schedule, I heard his story by telephone.

"I had a lot of responsibilities, being the man. I had to make all the arrangements because my wife was dealing with the effects of having given birth. We were new in town so we did not have any support. So I grieved much later. One day as I sat in the tub I cried like a baby.

"You see, I am the man, I have to deal with this. I'm supposed to be the stabilizing force although I felt totally devastated. I needed to be alone for a while. We abide in a culture that tells us not to show or express sadness. We are expected to remain strong in the face of adversity, and we withhold a show of emotions to a great extent. I am still old school in my beliefs. No two people are alike because I have seen some very emotional men.

"A lot of men are different. I am not your typical example of a male. Mary's grief was much more apparent in her external self. I kind of sublimated mine."

Jacob

Jacob cried during most of the interview. This was the second death experience for him, the first involved the couple's stillborn daughter, Lucy.

"It was hard the night of John's death. We were seeing babies being born, babies crying, and being delivered. It seemed to me that they could have put us in a special room. I must have heard four or five babies being born.

"My friends and relatives seemed to think that our experience should be over in about two to three months, but that's not the way it really is. I think about John every day just about every two hours, maybe more. See Pat has friends she can talk to. Every time I try to bring the subject up with people I know, they just change the subject. You always need somebody to talk to. But then, how do you bring it up?

"I wish now that I had held John. It is harder for me now than it was then. I feel the grief more now. It seems to me that I was always busy then. I need something to ease the hurt."

Thompson

I met Thompson following a support group meeting. We arranged a time for a telephone interview. When I called at the scheduled time, even though we had limited prior contact, he jokingly said, I thought you had forgotten about me.

He tried to mask it, but I knew that he cried throughout the interview. If I had acknowledged his tears, it could have been the end of our conversation.

"I wish we had a picture of Rachel. After she was buried, I asked why hospital personnel didn't take a picture. The doctor said, "You wouldn't want that."

"It's been sometime now, and I've been giving, giving, and giving; nobody gives to me. You know, I need help. I need somebody to tell me that I'm being loved, that they care about me. You know, I feel like I am being left out.

"I'm the one who is doing everything else, but I am left out of everything--even with my friends. I feel like I don't have a right to talk about this. As soon as I do, they turn off. They turn their backs on me. My best friends wouldn't even talk to me. They treated me as though they were saying, "Your wife had the pain of birth, you have no pain because she carried the baby."

"I often thought that my wife needed to have seen Rachel. Since she died, I have had an empty feeling. It was just like somebody put their hands in my body and took my heart out. At the time, I didn't know how to ask for what I needed. I needed help, but I didn't know how to ask for it. I was never taught how to ask for help.

"It's hard for a man when he loses a baby because everybody asks, "How is your wife doing?" They never ask about you. You know what? It hurts. I mean, true, I love my wife, and I love for people to ask me how she is doing, but I would like for somebody to ask about me, too. "How do you feel about your baby dying? Can I be of some help to you?"

"I need help and support, too. I loved the child as much as my wife. People must learn to realize that. Since Rachel died, I have asked people in similar situations if they need someone to talk to. It helps to talk about it."

Roberto

I interviewed Roberto following a support group meeting.
He cried as he relived the life and death of Carmen.

"The first six weeks our families were very sympathetic. After that they told my wife, "You know, it is time for you to get over it."

"Some of them even thought after two or three months we should be grief free. Not just relatives, but other people too. I said, 'You just can't. Look, it is going to take sometime.' Most of the people felt Carmen is dead and buried and that it is better because she only lived one day.

"One thing I hated was when they said, "You are young, you can have more children." I hated it when people said that to me. And another thing, I got upset about is that they always asked, "How is Maria doing?" Never, how am I doing.

"The main thing I hated was when people said to me, "You are young enough now, you can just have other children." They acted like Carmen didn't exist.

"I live a long way from work. So early in the morning the thoughts start me on that lonesome road again. I always think about it. I have been in a daze. I feel as though I am missing something. I remember wanting to stay busy, seemed like I couldn't be busy enough."

Don

I scheduled an interview with Don following a support group meeting in his home city. The flow of conversation was totally unrestrained.

"I sort of just put one foot in front of the other and kind of walked through those days almost as if I was in a daze. I don't know. I had to undergo therapy about three months after Joanne died. I had sort of a delayed grief reaction.

"On the surface, our relationship wasn't so stormy. Below the surface, our relationship did change. It is twice as good now though. We are more open with each other. We communicate openly, even on negative subjects.

"I think about Joanne daily. I felt guilty when she died because I thought our sexual intercourse in the latter part of the third trimester had caused her death. When she died, I just wanted to be with my wife."

Carl

It was difficult for Carl to share his experience. I paused several times during the interview because Carl left the room to cry.

"We didn't name her. We just called her *Little One*. Nobody encouraged us to name her. I wish we had. We had a name picked out, but we thought we would save it. I hate we didn't go ahead.

"The nurses were understanding. They were fantastic, but the doctor, oh boy. He came in 12 hours after *Little One*'s death and told Betty, "You can go home now." He left the room right after he said that.

"Well, one friend was excellent. He came over at 3:00AM and talked to me. I could talk to him a few times after that. Other friends avoided me. I really wanted to bring the subject up, but I felt like I had to protect my friends from what was going on with me. I just wish now that I was more honest with myself.

"I used to think about *Little One* all the time. I felt isolated and angry when she died.

"They asked me right away about funeral arrangements. I was still trying to grasp what had been said. They looked at me funny when I was slow to respond. I just needed time before I could deal with everything."

Wallace

Wallace's wife, Kay, was present for part of the interview. She spoke freely about her relationship with Wallace, and their experience with death. Wallace would nod his head and smile. It seemed that Kay knew him well. Wallace was just as expressive.

"Oh, I guess, if you're not weeping or you're not crying or whatever, people think you don't care. Inside, you know, people don't know what's happening inside a person. They just see what's outside. You're not going to let them know what's happening inside of you. It doesn't mean that you're okay.

"I guess what I experienced is all a part of being a man. It seems that 90% of the people I came in contact with would say to me, "How is the wife taking it?"

"It was just like a sore on my finger; it was there and I know it wasn't going to go away in one day. I think about my baby. If I go to the store or other place, I'll go by the cemetery. I won't tell Kay.

"I often think of my baby being in heaven. I can't explain how I felt. Kay was on medication. She would wake up and ask for our baby. I would tell her what had happened. She would go to sleep, wake up and ask the same thing. This went on and on. I didn't know what to do or say. I just wanted to be recognized for being human I guess."

119

Derrick

When Derrick opened the door and acknowledged my presence, his eyes told of his words to come. Initially, he was reluctant to talk.

"The only reason I agreed to this interview is that my mother told me to do it. I don't talk to anybody about my feelings, no strangers anyway. Since you're here, I'll talk to you.

"I tried to control my feelings, I mean, I figure it's more like a gift from God to be able to do so. Everybody can't control their feelings. I mean it is really hard. I believe, I catch more hell controlling my feelings than I would if I just express what is on my mind. I think about how other people might react. Maybe it would cause another conflict. So I just drop it like it is, and prevent an argument.

"Seems like people ought to know. You know the man has got to be hurting. He just had a baby to die. They should just do whatever they honestly can do for him. They should do it, and try to do a little bit more. I tell you right now, I wanted to kill myself.

"I often wonder what Bryan would have been like growing up. I had big plans for him you know. When he died, I remember being scared, because I really didn't know what to do. I just needed a shoulder to lean on."

Charles

I met Charles at his office. It was a very difficult interview to conduct. Although Charles did not hesitate when I approached him for his story, he did not share his experience easily. He would respond; however, I literally worked to obtain each response.

"I am still angry about how the whole thing was handled. I really don't think the doctors and nurses did what they really could to save Chuck. Actually, I thought about suing, but my wife wouldn't let me.

"I kept thinking that this is not the way things are supposed to happen. I felt as though I could hardly make it. I felt as though I needed to talk to someone. People don't care. At the same time, I wanted insincere people to leave me alone. We had enough to deal with. We blamed ourselves for Roger's death and had a lot of marital problems."

Jim

I interviewed Jim in his home. It was difficult for him to share his experience. The outcome of the interview suggested a need for continued support and a follow-up system.

"It is such a sensitive thing; it's hard to deal with. I really wouldn't know how to help another father, because I didn't, and don't know how to help myself.

"I felt as though I was to blame for Kyle's death. With my feelings, I hurt but I never cry. The best thing for me is to keep my mind off of it.

"But inside, I got a lot of things going on inside me that I can't put in words. I've never been one to talk a lot. So I just try to stay busy."

Jeff

Jeff agreed to share his story by phone. It was very difficult for him to recount the events of his twins' life and death. He cried throughout the interview. The death of his twins was very recent. Pauses during our conversation were allowed as Jeff needed them.

"The doctors and nurses were the best people to talk to. They gave me a lot of comfort. I could be myself. They understood what I was going through. They braced me for what people would say. All of that helped me deal with their deaths.

"But I still didn't know what was going on. I just sort of walked around. Sometimes I couldn't control my feelings, and I just lost it.

"When it happened, I kept trying to figure out what had happened. I was in shock more than anything. I just walked around in a daze. I remember thinking that people can say some dumb things at a really bad time. I needed my friends though, and they avoided me when I needed them most."

Parker

The time lapse since Kirk's death did not alter Parker's reconstruction of the experience. He did not hesitate to express what other fathers had difficulty saying.

"I didn't know how people were supposed to react and what people were supposed to do. I hadn't had that much association with death. But, I got to thinking, that I will never be able to spend a day like this with Kirk.

"I felt angry because I couldn't do anything about the death. I was angry and frustrated. I wanted to hold Kirk and say something to him even though he died.

"At the time the child dies, it is very important for the father to hold him. If not then, before, if he can. Say something to him. No matter what it is, it doesn't even have to make sense, just do it.

"You won't get that chance again. You'll always wonder and want to do something if you don't.

"I was very angry with God at one time. One day, I was out cutting wood; it was a very beautiful day. I was by myself and I got to thinking about the fact that I would never be able to spend a day like this with Murphy. I just raised my fist to the sky and yelled at God. I told Him that He didn't have the right to take Murphy's life like that. If anybody has done anything wrong, it's me.

"I had lived longer, and he should have done something

to me or caused me to die or something. Let the baby live. Later, I felt bad about doing that. My brother-in-law told me that it was okay and that God understood."

Ralph

My presence did not seem to hinder Ralph's need to cry as he relived the life and death of Christopher.

"Helen had taken fertility drugs for so long. We were so happy. We had been trying. So I felt like we had been cheated, and Christopher may have been our only chance.

"I will always feel that some things went on in that nursery that we were not told about. We left Christopher's side one day and went home, but we sat by the phone constantly. We called the nursery and one of the nurses had dropped an IV bag on his hand. They said a small cut was on his hand. We rushed up to the hospital. And the small cut turned out to be about one and a half inches. We felt that if they passed that off what else are they passing off. They finally seemed to understand our needs and allowed us to touch him. They offered to let us hold him, but we were afraid. I wish they had been more persistent.

"Helen and I were afraid to hold him--just scared. We thought that if we picked him up it would end his life. The nurses offered, but we could not. It tears me up when I think about it. I just needed answers to my questions.

"My parents always taught me to say what I feel no matter what anyone thinks. Just the other night, it seemed the right thing to do. I started crying. It was natural for me, but others around me were uncomfortable."

James

James told me that he had been waiting for someone to ask about his feelings following the death of Karen. The interview was held in his home. In spite of all the noise and neighborhood children running back and forth, James shared his experience as though they were not present.

"When Karen died, I would have liked for my wife to know that I needed her to hold me, hug me, and take care of me. I did it for her. But no, she couldn't. I mean we could hold and hug each other, but we weren't comforting each other because we both hurt so badly. But I knew I had to be strong for her, and I was.

"I remember thinking that people don't know me. I understand how I react in a lot of situations, and what is really going on inside me are not necessarily the same in a lot of cases. Everybody has that macho thing. It depends on who I am around. When I think I have dealt with my emotions, *wham*, there is that brick wall up again.

"I tell you right now, I felt like I had been stabbed to the quick. I just needed to be able to admit that I felt intensely bad. I needed to let the emotions run their course and then think about it, or whatever."

Dennis

I interviewed Dennis by phone. I met him at a support group meeting. He talked freely and suggested that support groups are not for everybody. He said that a group for fathers only would work better for him.

"I really didn't feel like working for a few days. Actually a couple of weeks. I would go into the church office, and do just what I had to do, and leave. I had to get back into working. Fortunately for me, I had been there a long time, so, everybody kind of took care of the day-to-day stuff.

"My step-dad is wonderful so there was no pressure for me to get back to work. When things would get really bad, I would just go off somewhere by myself.

"I didn't want to believe that there was something wrong with my baby. Carrie had to work so hard at breathing. She wasn't getting better; it was almost a relief when she died. At least, she wasn't suffering. I hurt, but I hurt more for her.

"When Carrie died, I needed someone to tell me how to talk to my wife. I didn't know how to let her know how I felt."

Kenny

When I talked with Kenny, I discovered that he had experienced death of more than one child. He was baffled as he shared his anger, disappointment, and his grief.

"I mean, it's an experience I wouldn't wish on my worst enemy. It is very draining emotionally and physically. I could hardly put one foot in front of the other. I mean it tears you apart to see your child die. To survive it, you should take things one day at a time, an hour at a time, a minute at a time, and a second at a time.

"When it happened, even though I had quit smoking maybe five years ago, I felt myself digging in my pockets for cigarettes. Everything just kind of caved in after that. I have to admit that I got involved with my work. It is one of my best escapes.

"(Laughing with tears rolling down his face.) Even though we have gone through this more than one time, I don't think our relatives and friends understand it at all. I don't care if you term one baby as being a miscarriage; it was our baby. But for a stillborn, to get so close and boom. It is so hard to deal with feelings. The suffering is so hard.

"I wanted to be in on decisions. I don't need anybody thinking for me."

Harry

Harry chuckled nervously throughout the interview. At times, he laughed so often, I found it difficult to follow him as he attempted to recount his story. Laughter on his face and tears in his eyes.

"I don't know what I would have done or how I would have made it without my faith in God. My church family was very supportive of me. My faith gave me strength.

"It helped us to get closer to the Lord. My wife and I got along okay before Dan's death, and after, it seemed to draw us even closer to each other. In some support group meetings you hear about how couples are splitting up. It will tear you apart. You have to let the other person know what is happening inside of you. It'll come out all wrong if you don't. It was hard, but I did it.

"I always felt so alone when I visited Dan. I needed the nurses to talk to me more and tell me about what was going on."

David

David was very expressive. To make a point, he would stop and laugh nervously. Then he would continue. He said that he remembers being surprised by his reaction at the time of his baby's death.

"I walked the halls and watched things going on. I didn't know what else to do. So I just went through the motions. In other words, I kept observing until it was over.

"When Cedric died, I felt like I had lost a really good friend. We had actually been together for so long during the pregnancy. We'd think that he would possibly make it, and then he would slide all the way back down to being critical. It was like being on a roller coaster.

"I got to see him look at us. He would grasp my finger. So I got to know him at least. I wouldn't trade that for anything. I lost something that can never be replaced.

"I just wished the hospital would have just gone on ahead and took pictures. They should let parents know after the wife is discharged that if they wish, the pictures are there. I would love to have had some pictures of Cedric. I went back up right after he died to get his hat. I think they had already gotten rid of it. They just don't realize how important that hat was to me.

"I felt cheated by my friends they really weren't there. I wanted to talk with someone who had experienced this."

131

Herschel

My meeting with Herschel took place at his office. He was very conservative with his responses, at first. Later, he seemed to forget I was present and talked freely.

"When Carla died, I didn't feel like doing much of anything. I had to sign some papers for the autopsy. Of course, my parents and best friends were there and that helped. Immediately afterwards, we seemed to drift apart. I actually felt cheated by my friends.

"My sister convinced us to go to a support group. I went, but that is not what I wanted. They sit around in this huge circle, and you're supposed to be strong and kind of express your feelings. I still can't express my emotions in front of a group of people.

"I have tried a lot of things to help with the feelings. I was raised in the church, but I have been involved with different things like drugs. I still think about Carla each and every day. It used to be every minute especially the first few months.

"The only thing that seemed to help was for me to go by the cemetery and be alone. I then came to understand that children are gifts from God. You always think that you will not outlive your children and that is just the way it is supposed to be. Not the other way around."

Sal

I met Sal at his home for the interview. I could see that he had a lot to deal with emotionally. His eyes shouted what he attempted to hide.

"My whole family and Margie's parents were there. They were very supportive. I don't know what time it was. They took care of me and Margie. We just floated along.

"Even with all of that, it was still kind of like a deflating thing. I felt just like a balloon that had no air in it. Just like someone had sucked all of the air out of me.

"I had my hopes up, and all of a sudden everything was taken away from me. You have no control over any of that. I felt like such a failure to my wife and to myself.

"It did feel really good to hold Joseph. I felt if we had belonged to a church then we could have had church members come by and help us through this and administer the baptism. I know he is in heaven. I believe he is growing just like he would had he lived. Right now, he would be walking maybe talking. I think of him like that.

"Being in a support group has helped. By being a part of the group, I know that someone else can kind of understand what I how I feel. I am a poor talker. I am talking more now.

"Margie is pregnant again, and I am scared. I don't want the same thing to happen. I don't know what I would do if it did. I just can't relax."

Bob

I interviewed Bob at his church after a rehearsal. It seemed as though we were not strangers. He shared his story freely.

"I was so frustrated and tired. I went back to work after about a week. My employer pulled me to the side and said, "Don't worry about it. I had the same thing happen to me, you've just got to go on and get on with your life. It's not like it was alive."

"I suppose he was concerned, but he made me feel worse. The only friend I have that would really talk to me did not say much, but he listened a lot.

"Other people asked me what happened to cause the death. When I tried to tell them they acted like they really didn't want to know. They didn't want any details.

"I was in a great shock when I first heard. Everything seemed to pile in at one time. I felt like I was in a dream, and that it cannot be happening. I had this tough unfeeling image on the outside, but on the inside I was screaming. I felt like someone was tearing my insides out, it felt kind of rough."

John

John smiled as he told of how Emmit responded to his voice when he talked to him in the nursery. He also cried as he spoke of their relationship.

"You see, I used to talk to him when my wife was pregnant. We had a special relationship. He recognized my voice. My son was a fighter. He tried for so long. I was proud of him.

"My wife needed a lot of attention because of her illness, so I had to be strong. The doctors didn't think she would carry Emmit as long as she did. I was so busy taking care of everything, I did not have time for me. Later, I do remember feeling like I had been hit by a bolt of lightning.

"I remember thinking, what do I do now? This cannot be happening. I felt like my whole world had been ripped apart. I wanted someone to talk to me, someone to listen to me, maybe someone who had been through this before."

13

Perspective

I *don't need anyone to tell me how I should feel. I need
to tell somebody and have them listen.*

These words were echoed by almost every father
who shared his story. Listening should be emphasized as an
art form. There is no need for people to become experts on
the topic of death simply because someone is grieving.
Listening is the only requirement.

Fathers offer a silent appeal for recognition of what
actually exists for them as they grieve. They want someone
to hear what they have to say. From the interviews included,

it is evident that information from studies on grief may not represent a true picture of the phenomenon as described by fathers.

Stage theorists caution that people progress during grief at their own pace. One cannot set time limits for any stage. However, because stage theorists also discuss pathological grief and some mention time limits for normal grief, people often focus on that pronounced length of time.

In the original study, information obtained from fathers suggests that classic stages of grief, for them, require re-examination. What fathers described first is *a sense of duty*. Whether performance of duty occurs because of socialization to their role or because it is a method of flight from emotions is not the issue. Their performance of duty requires recognition.

Safety, comfort, and expectations are terms that possibly describe fathers as they perform official business of signing papers and arranging for the burial of their newborn. Some nurses, physicians, family members, and friends are guilty of turning to fathers for answers as they deal with a distraught mother and their own devastation.

Fathers who seem okay at the time do not always show behavior that provides a true depiction of actual feelings. These fathers handle details, and they appear comfortable with duties. However, their attachment to the baby is often forgotten by other people.

As expected, couple communications turn into a complex compilation of repressed emotions that become increasingly difficult to resolve. Unfortunately for some couples, instead of rallying together, they grow apart when one partner's feelings are not acknowledged. (See Part VI: *Resolutions*.)

PART V: PIECES

Each part fits, like pieces of a puzzle

14

Disclosure

Two children are overheard on a playground as they banter back and forth.

"Say it!"

"No, you go first."

"You go first," says Dana.

"No way, you will cheat. You go first," declares Max.

The two playmates continue this kind of dialog for some time. Each child tries to reassure the other that it is okay to bare their souls. Perhaps the playmates, like so many adults, have a heart-rendering secret to share. Or maybe it's simply a vestige of childhood that we all inherit, causing the two to squabble.

At first, most adults would find this conversation foolish for such yearnings of honesty. How quickly we forget our youth. Nevertheless, even children know that sharing too many secrets is not without risks.

From early childhood, we learn that if too much is shared, the listener gains the advantage of knowing some prized portion of our world, once known only to us.

Or! Whoever goes first can lie, gain the confidence of the other person, and cause that person to disclose closely guarded secrets while the listener does not.

So, it is in childhood that we first learn about disclosure. When it does occur, tradeoffs exist and relationships emerge at a new level for the participating parties. Is it ever acceptable to share emotions without recourse? One instance occurs when both parties are involved in the welfare of another - for example, in a loving relationship. Thus, a pregnant couple should relate honestly with each other.

In most cultures, women are encouraged to verbalize their feelings. Consequently, women are often more relationship-oriented. A woman will usually disclose her needs and emotions first. This approach is an unveiling strategy that hopefully will precipitate a similar pattern from their mates. However, reciprocal disclosure may not occur. It is certain that limited disclosure and stagnant communication decrease feelings of security between partners in a relationship.

Disclosure propels a relationship of any kind to a new dimension. It bares the soul and unloads the heart of burdens too heavy to endure. As would be expected, it clears the air and brings honesty to a new level.

If disclosure is so good for you, then why don't people engage in uncensored discussions with each other? And why doesn't it occur for serious topics as often as it does for superficial conversations about politics or food?

First, disclosure is a phenomenon that requires participating parties to share openly and honestly. Hesitation occurs as the fear of retribution frightens us regarding a particular topic. However, one involved party must determine the level of honesty for the pair.

Will one person be more honest than the other? What are the consequences of being dishonest, and if one person is not self-revealing, how will you ever know the truth? Will the disclosed information meet the listener's expectations?

One fact is certain. In an intimate relationship, if honest disclosure does not occur during times of stress, conflict is inevitable. Grief causes catastrophic stress. Both parents must find strength in each other. It is natural for both parents to recount events that led to the baby's death. However, sharing is halted and the relationship becomes strained when only one partner is able to reveal their emotions.

In most cases, the grieving couple's relationship centers around getting the less willing partner to talk. A standoff occurs. Usually it is the father who is reticent and frequently becomes withdrawn. Most fathers want to share the turmoil inside them. Nevertheless, it is common for months and years to pass before revelation of emotions occurs, if it occurs at all.

For years, as a nurse, I have interviewed parents and other informants who have volunteered that their mates avoided discussing the death of their child. This avoidance behavior spanned a period of 17 to 30 years. These women noticed differences in their mates' reactions on anniversary dates, and on occasions that would correspond with the child's developmental age: a graduation or wedding.

However, when women confronted their mates regarding their behavior, the men still refused to admit that their present expression of emotions had any connection with the dead baby. Maybe their mates were unable to associate behavioral changes to the long-ago death.

One woman shared these comments months after her husband's death.

"My husband is dead now. Our baby died 37 years ago at one month old. (Pause) We never discussed how he felt when the baby died. Now, I know that a side of him existed that I never knew."

In his book, *Disclosing Man to Himself*, Sidney Jourard writes that a man carefully selects the experiences he will disclose in words and behavior to whoever is nearby. He, then, becomes selective with disclosure.

His mate is increasingly aware of his lack of communication, particularly around friends and family who now seem superficial to him. She may wonder why. When asked, he refuses to explain his behavior. Eventually, their relationship begins to suffer.

It is essential for couples to engage in intensive relationship-building and communication restructuring following the death of a baby (see Chapter 20). That stressful time offers a couple opportunities to nurture and renew their relationship. Part VI, *Resolution,* includes activities that enhance healing without self-censure.

15

Control

C ontrol is a term fathers often use to indicate their independence, of being in charge and being the responsible man in their families. A father finds himself in a precarious position when faced with the death of his baby, and in other stressful situations. When he cannot control the outcome of events that surround pregnancy, he often questions his manhood.

In explaining control, fathers mentioned their fear of vulnerability and powerlessness. They were taught as children to shun any display of emotions that suggests loss of control. Yet, anger and rage at the appropriate time are two emotions that are not restricted for boys and men.

Being in control, as explained by them, is having *access to information* and having *one's finger on the pulse of what goes on in their environment.*

Or does it?

It would seem that control is a variable that is misplaced during times of grief. So being out of control, or loss of control, must be devastating to someone who normally has command of their existence.

Androgyny almost predicts a personality that is communicative, does not fear disclosure, and does not have a problem with suppressed emotions. This assumption was untrue with fathers who participated in the original study as informants. Instead, control permeated all sex-types.

According to the fathers interviewed, control describes a comfortable position for them in all life experiences. Fathers spoke of being out of control in some form following the death of their babies. Most of them admitted that they were uncomfortable with this feeling and attempted to avoid thinking about their immediate situation because of their fear of being out of control. Being task-oriented after a death is a father's attempt to bring order and control to his environment.

For fathers, control was used to describe two aspects of their lives:

(1) how they dealt with their emotions

(2) in normal situations, how they were able to direct and adjust life experiences in their immediate surroundings.

To cry in front of their mates would put them at risk for loss of control. Therefore, crying would cause their relationship role as the dominant, all-controlling male to be scrutinized and a topic for possible change.

Ted

"I tried to control my emotions. It's not that I was embarrassed or anything; it's just that somebody has to be in control when things like this happen. And then a lot of stuff builds up and it has to come out some kind of way. Something little might happen and all this frustration might erupt, and then you have to control that, too."

Allen

"When a man controls his feelings it comes back and boomerangs on him. Then it's twice as negative. We suppress our feelings better than women. I don't think we, or I, control my feelings any better than a woman. Men suppress feelings . . . and repress things too much."

Anger is closely aligned with being out of control for some fathers. Not being able to provide a solution was the cause of much frustration for them. Many fathers perceived that they were being disrespected by physicians and nurses. Therefore, their chances of gaining control were limited. Being out of control invokes feelings of helplessness, which often precipitate discomfort and rage.

There are rituals approved by society as ways men can express their emotions when they feel out of control. It has long been accepted for men to "lose it" at sporting events. Men who were once thought to be loners, then, become one of the boys. Some degree of intimacy is accepted.

Fighting is a way some men have expressed anger and feelings of being out of control. A man's aggression is more tolerated in society than his tears. Although drinking is not condoned, if it is viewed as a rationalization for a father's attempt to sort through the death of a baby, it too is more endured than a display of tears.

Tears from a man force others to think of the enormity of the given situation. Others must then think of their own mortality.

16

The Eyes Have It

There are many aspects of life that confound me. One is dark sunglasses. Some of them are so dark they are solid black. I do know that medical reasons exist for some wearers. People wear odd-shaped ones because of styles of the time. However, some people wear them to hide. From what? I don't have an answer for that question. But I interviewed numerous fathers who wore dark sunglasses on a cloudy day.

I like eyes. I have always liked them - mine and those of each and every person I meet. Of all the facial features that can represent a person's personality, their eyes cannot keep a secret. Eyebrows can deceive, a nose can pretend it likes what it smells, and lips will not tell. But give me eyes because they are windows of the soul. Whatever the heart feels, and the mouth cannot utter, the eyes express. This statement is so true for fathers I have interviewed over the years. Even the ones who chose to wear dark sunglasses. Regardless of how the person attempts to present a dense veneer, a person's eyes will give them away every time.

A person built like a gladiator has feelings identical to a person of smaller stature. An essential factor of those feelings is tolerance, attachment, and interpretation of the moment. However, society expects the gladiator to fit a specific category of descriptors. The small-framed person can display almost any kind of behavior because of descriptors assigned for that body frame.

I have interviewed fathers who indicated that their experience is different. Others denied having a problem with people who do not ask about them. One father said, "I could handle my own problems, and I got through it just fine." However, their eyes sent a conflicting message as though to voice what they could not. *He is lying, he is hurt. Can't you see he won't look directly at you? Look at how empty we appear.* After sharing my observations and messages from other fathers, the façade of being okay gave way to admission of actual feelings.

Crying eyes don't necessarily have tears that drip down

the face. Some eyes simply turn red. Some people cry and you hear sighs, whimpers, and sobs, while others can talk without any change in voice quality.

I suppose being a nurse has aided my ability to discern pain when joy is expressed. But the reality of any situation is that expected reactions exist for certain circumstances.

Regardless of race, gender, ethnic origin, religion, or sexual preference, certain consequences are anticipated following specific antecedents. For instance, most patients bleed during surgery, all people require air to live, all healthy people enjoy food in their mouths, and everyone experiences pain and suffering when someone significant to them dies--even men who are fathers.

It is not appropriate here to debate evidence of life for an unborn child. My statements bear no political support in the anti-abortion issue or of when life actually begins. My point is that when a couple discovers that they are pregnant, both people who want children and are in a healthy relationship are overwhelmed with joy.

I have observed this kind of joy innumerable times. Men play with unborn children by talking and caressing their mates' stomachs. Additionally, expectant parents have daydreams and night dreams about their unborn children. These children are given family features before they are ever born.

With these generally accepted facts in mind, why on earth do people ignore a baby's life when the baby dies during pregnancy, immediately following delivery, or even during the first year? It is often assumed after one look at a father who is not exhibiting the expected behavior that he must be okay.

In general, people are simply uncomfortable with their ability to face grief. So they often seem callous when giving messages of condolence. We do not know what to say, yet it is okay to express condolences to the mother. It is done without a word of regret to the father who, for all outward appearances, is doing fine, but he is caving in on the inside.

Remember, for every action there is a reaction. It is implausible for happiness to occur at the discovery of pregnancy and for easy acceptance to follow the initial announcement of death.

Men who appear stoic often have sad eyes that cry in private. Stop and think for a moment. Simply because you do not witness tears, it does not mean they do not occur for grieving fathers.

Crying during times of stress is tension-releasing. It is therapeutic. Fathers mentioned being aware of hindering tears, and being overwhelmed by the energy required to do so. Others mentioned that tears were a natural response when they were comfortable with people present and other factors in the environment.

17

Isolation

I t's not that I want to run away; it's just that I cannot deal
with my own feelings when I am around Karen. If she
starts to cry, then I forget about what's going on with
me. But I just need to get away for a few days and just sit
and do things alone and let it out."

"I can let my feelings out when I am by myself. That's
how I handle things. I don't want anybody around. Most of
the time I go by the cemetery."

Getting away for a few days or even a few hours was commonly expressed by fathers. Being alone was a normal practice for them in dealing with confusing or frustrating situations. They were the main support for their mates. They were the protectors. When their mates had dealt with their feelings, it was at that point that most fathers wanted to retreat to a private place to be alone to deal with their emotions.

Generally, isolation starts early in a man's life. It continues and is fostered because most men do not have a significant friendship with another man. When asked about their relationship with a specific man, it is not surprising to hear, "Oh, he is just someone I do things with. We're not that close."

When men are together in a group, it is common for them to continue the façade of being strong--keeping the image going. Even when the size of the group changes to two people, instead of allowing one person to air their feelings the other is often uncomfortable and the exchange does not occur.

Even men with the most engaging personalities, astounding gift of gab, and prosperous positions often do not have male friends with whom they share their problems. Fortunately, this is not true of all men.

Most single men belong to an exclusive male organization or fraternity. With marriage and fatherhood, some men will end those memberships. Social activities are aligned with like individuals--other married men. The opportunity to commune with a high school, college, or fraternity buddy decreases.

The isolation fathers sometime seek is a solution they have tried before when problem-solving. If it works for them, it should be supported. Afterwards, counseling is essential with their mate and individually to discuss feelings. However, if a person is confused, and questions their role in precipitating a birth, rehashing events alone is not a therapeutic solution.

But what choice do men have? Most men and fathers have no best friend outside their immediate family. So if their mate is that friend, and if she is not available because of her own grief, who do they turn to? This is a question men must ponder and then seek solutions.

The isolation or need to get away voiced by fathers centered around knowing how they felt even though their feelings were difficult to express. These fathers simply wanted time to cry, scream, yell, curse, hit something, and contemplate their future alone, without someone constantly talking or asking them to express their grief. Fathers also mentioned that after getting away, they could return to their situation and be more productive.

Some fathers who worked in white-collar jobs, and especially prosperous businessmen in the study, were able to enjoy a week or longer away from home and work. These fathers either arranged a trip or participated in a prearranged outing without their mates. Less affluent fathers were not able to afford this kind of luxury. However, fishing with the guys or alone worked.

Most wives viewed their mates' requests for time away as an opportunity to escape reality and a desire to be rid of them. However, this was not the original intent. Most wives voiced that they felt insecure in their relationships when their mates could not explain their need to be away without them.

18

Hit Me

it me! I'm bad.
    Hold on!
    This chapter is not a review of soul singer James Brown's lyrics. It is an opportunity to share the language of grief that fathers use to describe their feelings. Men are more graphic in their descriptions than women. It is common for men to use terminologies associated with action to express their feelings.

If you ask a mother how she felt when her baby died, she will provide a description using a terminology that is commonly accepted for grief. A familiar association is made that others understand.

A father who provides that same description will give you a picture of another event. For example, most fathers gave the following response when asked to describe their feelings: "I felt like someone had beat the hell out of me." Generally, mothers will tell you, "I was so distraught, just shocked and overwhelmed with anger." Few fathers will give a similar response.

"Hit me" were words used to show acknowledgment of the death. "When it hit me," or "it hit me." This expression is interpreted to mean, "When I finally realized the truth." Another frequently used description for feelings is: "It felt like someone tore my insides out."

Fathers rarely used descriptions that actually appear in textbooks. Body responses of increased heartbeats and sensations of numbness were described as "someone ripped my heart out," or of "being ripped apart," and "like someone took my heart out of my body." The last description was used by fathers to indicate decreased realization of an actual heart rate.

A father described his immediate feelings as "stabbed to the quick." He became so distraught during the interview that he ended it before I could ask for clarification. During a subsequent interview, a father had difficulty describing his feelings. I asked him, "Is it anything like being stabbed to the quick?"

He looked surprised and said with enthusiasm, "That's exactly how I felt." He added, "It's like somebody "cuts you to the core." With this additional information, I then realized that he felt as though the center of his body had been cut to the point of severe pain.

A large percentage of fathers had an urge to hit somebody or something. Release of built-up frustration is key here. It is not that a large percentage of fathers in the study were violent, but throughout their lifetime, emphasis was placed on physical activity and control. Moreover, irritating or threatening situations in most of their lives were sometimes managed in a physical way.

If you overstep your boundary, a man will put you in your place. If you do not respect his position, an altercation is possible, whether physical or verbal.

Fathers who described a need to hit somebody usually felt out of control or disrespected in the hospital, unacknowledged as the head of their households. They acknowledged their limited understanding of medicine. Their emphasis on involvement was not an attempt to prevent the physicians and nurses from caring for their babies.

Their description of immediate feelings as "wanting to hit someone" is associated with periods of having control taken away from them. This involved not being given information, being told to wait outside, "We'll get to you later," "you would not understand," and "you're in the way here." The greatest feeling of inadequacy occurred when fathers thought that someone was negligent, and they were unwilling to accept that there was nothing more that could have been done for their baby.

A man's manner of describing his feelings may be unfamiliar to his mate. When she asks how he felt when their baby died, if he describes his feelings as "being hit with a bolt of lightning," her next statement might be, "How did you really feel?" In other words, "Use terms I understand."

An example of a conversation between a grieving couple follows.

> "Honey [or] Baby [some term of endearment], tell me how you actually felt." Again, the father uses a description that clearly represents his feelings from his perspective. "I felt like I was floating around in a void."

This kind of conversation took place with Linda and Warren. In tears, Linda turned to Warren and said, "I don't understand why you can't just tell me how you felt." Warren responded, "I told you, and I am not telling you anymore." Then he left the room.

After this conversation ("that went nowhere," according to Linda), she called a friend to relate her distress of not getting Warren to open up. The friend agreed. "I know what you mean. I asked my husband about something that happened, and he started talking nonsense."

It is clear that a man's way of describing his feelings is

sometimes confusing for his mate. My point: it is a dire necessity for couples to learn about each other, especially their communication pattern during a crisis. However, some needs are difficult to predict. It is essential, though, for each partner to understand the pattern of communication when both partners are together as a couple and as individuals.

Couples frequently become intimate strangers following their baby's death. Often, one person claims to experience a greater degree of frustration. Whatever exists in the relationship, both partners experience stress when communication is halted.

A father's way of describing his grief deserves recognition. In attempting to understand the language they use to describe their grief, we can begin to learn more about fathers and their emotions.

19

Cowboys Don't Live Here Anymore - A Matter of Respect

Movies have influenced our lives since the world gave in to television. Past and present roles played by men in family systems are easily traced through cowboy pictures. It is there that men have come full circle with their emotional lives.

Have you seen an old-time cowboy picture lately? Men were always characterized in cowboy pictures as masters of anything outside the home.

In these pictures, cowboys are depicted as macho men who could ride a horse and catch a bad guy like a flash of lightning. They wore guns and tall hats and drank liquor at the town saloon. However, if you analyze those old cowboy pictures, you will find one point of life they just could not conquer: any affair of the heart.

Let's revisit a scene from one that shows chivalry in the midst of a brawl. I can see the old cowboys now.

"Howdy partner, new around these parts?" asks Cowboy Joe.

"Who's askin'?" demands Tex as he slowly positions himself near the stranger.

"Me, that's who, and you'd better be answering or you'll find yourself getting up out of the dirt."

"Oh yeah, you and who else?"

The two men ready themselves for a real knock-down drag-out fight.

A female customer enters the store.

Almost on cue, both men control their rage at the same time and pose like gentlemen.

There is a natural pause in conversation.

Both men tip their hats and smile.

The woman looks at both men, smiles, and nods her head as she acknowledges their presence. She looks around the store for a few minutes and makes a purchase. She walks out of the store. Again on cue, when the two men are sure the woman is out of hearing range, a brawl ensues.

During this era, and in old cowboy pictures, when men were portrayed in their homes they were usually eating dinner. When a baby was being born, their duties were to boil water and pace outside a closed door. If they encountered a problem that wasn't related to roping and steering, they were depicted alone brooding, especially over a lost love.

Times have changed, even in cowboy pictures produced today. It is not unusual to see a cowboy cook, clean, and ponder his emotional needs, and to want respect as a man, a father, and as a human being.

Like cowboys, fathers are also heroes. From the interviews, it is apparent that fathers want their emotional needs acknowledged. However, they are unlike long-ago cowboys on TV who lived their lives almost totally devoid of feelings, drinking away the pain, never to resolve their problems.

Instead of keeping females in their lives guessing about their feelings, fathers are seeking consolation, and some even provide answers. Yes, the old cowboy image is fading fast as today's men announce: "We don't want your pity, you still may not see us cry, but please respect our pain."

The real issue for them is for their mates and others in their immediate environment to at least acknowledge that they are human beings. They, too, are parents, and yes, they want recognition that they are still men. It's all about respect.

PART VI: RESOLUTION

Give sorrow words, the grief that does not speak
Whispers the o'er fraught heart and bids it break.

Shakespeare, Macbeth, Act IV, Sc. 3, 1623

20

Theory of Grief for Fathers

A theory of grief for fathers is not complete without
mentioning the terms "concept" and "paradigm." A
concept is an idea, something conceived, an
abstraction. A paradigm is a method of approaching or doing
the idea which is generally accepted as *the way*.

Grief is a concept. The act of grieving is a paradigm.
Both terms have been discussed for centuries in the
scientific community as humans attempt to provide meaning
to their existence. Also, each term is used to attach meaning
to a phenomenon in nature.

173

Changes in the way an idea is perceived, or its utility in explaining events in nature parsimoniously determine if the paradigm requires reassessment. When paradigms no longer fit, a paradigm *shift* occurs.

In his writings on theory construction, Paul Reynolds explains that *shifts* in ways of thinking will occur. Thomas Kuhn posed the basic premise that radical change in theory occurs when scholars debate the utility of a theory. Both philosophies suggest that as changes occur in nature, scientific explanations that predict behavior will also change as discoveries are made.

Scholars debate whether science is evolutionary or revolutionary. Evolutionists believe science develops in a straight line process with successive generations contributing to the body of known facts. Revolutionists contend that scientific development occurs sporadically in a zigzag fashion. An anomaly or crisis occurs. The theory does not quite explain events. Accepted thought is altered significantly. *Shifts* in thought occur and a new *way or approach* is taken.

As society develops and fathers assert their roles within the family, speculation about their behavior also will shift. Attributes germane to their new way of reacting are then attached to existing theory. A *shift* occurs in practice of the theory and knowledge increases. Grief is an example.

Families as Systems

Ludwig von Bertalanffy, a general systems theorist, explains man's interactions as a constant exchange of matter in an open environment. He also explains that a system is more than the sum of its parts.

A family is a system. Each member is an element or part of the whole. As family roles are realized and the family attempts to function as a unique system, each member's status and ability to function in that role must be considered. For each member to develop and prosper as a functioning element in a positive way, role ambiguity must be clarified. This requirement is essential for continued existence of the whole unit: the family, the system.

When a baby dies, the family experiences a definite setback in its growth plans. The family cannot progress until both parents and siblings resolve their grief for the dead child. With this, the system breaks down and the family unit cannot function optimally.

Grief Resolution

Many elements dictate the outcome of normal grief. The first element affected by grief is the "private self." The mind interprets a precipitating event. Attachment to an object in life experiences affects how the griever will respond. *Private self* is composed of beliefs, values, interpretations, and internalization of norms to derive the individual.

Inner turmoil or private self is represented by the "public self." Symptoms of grief are depicted first by facial cues. Moments later, the body participates. The person may become limp. The public self is influenced by societal norms and the private self: The manner in which cues of grief are displayed.

Both private self and public self are enhanced or detracted by significant *people* in the environment. People who are relatives and friends can assist a person who has difficulty with expression. Significant people help to refute ambiguity between societal norms and role performance by being supportive, providing a safe and approving environment for grief to occur. In essence, a person who has difficulty grieving is given permission to grieve when internalized norms conflict with the precipitating event - death of a baby.

Grief is either positive or negative. Grief that occurs naturally is positive. The grieving person allows their emotions to surface, and they ventilate feelings. In time, memories of the dead person will not evoke tears or overwhelming moods of stagnation.

On the other hand, negative grief is pathological. In this case, the person who experiences a death postpones dealing with the actual loss for an undetermined length of time. Depression and inability to continue life often occur years after the death.

Grief resolution is a continuous state. Evidence of its expression and resolution are balanced in man on gender influences and social support. When the griever operates in an open system with support persons and access to supportive groups, grief continues its natural course.

Interactions with other individuals and agencies are a common practice in open families (Figure 1). Members of the immediate family system gather resources from extended family members and the community to solve problems. In the initial stage of problem solving, solutions are attempted within the immediate environment. Disclosure occurs for resolution of grief and other identified problems. Balance and harmony are evident.

When the environment is closed and support people and facilities are not available, grief exists almost in a vacuum. People involved remain stagnant. Stereotypical gender identification often aligns a person against acknowledging emotions. Stagnation is inevitable and suppression of emotions occurs.

Interactions with family members and contact with community agencies for assistance to resolve problems are absent (Figure 2). Members of the immediate system deal with personal problems in isolation. Outsiders, or other environmental influences, are not considered. Social agencies are viewed in a suspicious manner. Individual family members attempt to manage problems without assistance. The cycle continues without immediate resolution of grief or other problems.

Grieving Patterns of Couples

Incongruent grief is apparent for most couples. It occurs at any point following the experience of death. This kind of grief is evident when one mate proceeds through the grief process with assistance of the other partner. Later, one partner interprets the behavior of the supporting partner and makes a judgement about how the person should have responded. No validation of behaviors is made with the person being judged.

Most mothers exhibit grieving behavior immediately. For fathers, the actual experience of grief is deferred because of role performance. Fathers perform duties, taking care of family needs and attending to details of the immediate situation. These men become preoccupied with a flurry of activities.

After the baby's burial, and long after their mates recover physically and emotionally, fathers often want time alone to deal with their own needs. They are unable to explain their reaction and manner of dealing with their emotions. Most of them are unable to voice their seemingly bizarre desire to *get away.*

Grief Reactions

Philosophers on grief have divided reactions into stages that are recognized around the world (Chapter 5, Grief). First, a person normally responds to an announcement of the death of a loved one with denial and shock. C. M. Parkes described this phase as "preoccupation." His description is more aligned with the initial reaction of fathers.

Fathers become preoccupied with completing tasks and making sure arrangements are made. Often, their initial grief is *delayed* until a less critical time.

Comments

A theory of grief for fathers should consider influences of gender differences and social support. In the future, the language of grief for fathers must be easily recognized. Role function and performance of duties deserve special attention in quantitative as well as qualitative studies when fathers are subjects.

The influence of control, isolation, language, nonverbal cues, and disclosure on a father's ability to grieve is important to future research. Other elements that facilitate the grieving process are significant and should be considered.

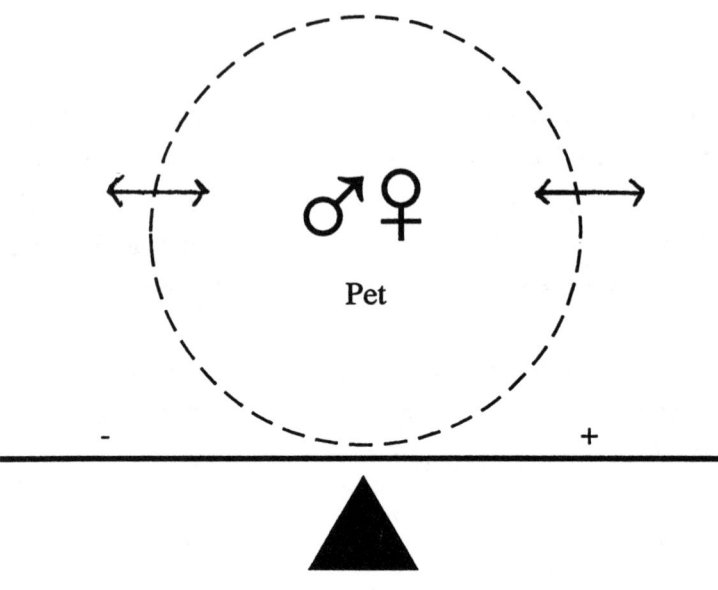

Pet

−   +

Figure 1.   Grief - Open Family System

- Interaction among fmily members
- Significant people are welcomed
- Support from community agencies
- Balance exists between gender influences and social support

+   Grief resolution progresses in time

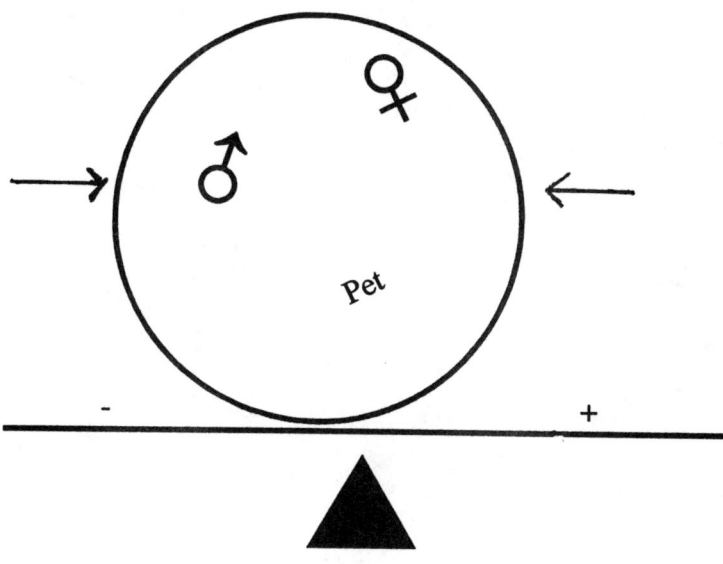

Figure 2. Grief - Closed Family System

- Difficult for others to interact with family members
- Family turmoil is present
- Absence of community resources
- Conflict with gender influences and social support

- Grief is usually unresolved or occurs with difficulty

21

Couple Communications

I wanted Kacy to realize that I needed to be hugged, too."

"Did you tell her?"

"No, I didn't."

"Why not?"

"She didn't have to tell me that she needed to be hugged, so why should I have to tell her? It's my baby, too. And I wanted him just as much as she did. All she seemed to think about was herself."

"Lisa and I have been married nine years. She is the only person I have felt close to. Before we were married, I had girlfriends, but I was never as close to them as I am to Lisa. She was different. After our baby died, it's just like our whole life changed.

"We sit there and just stare at each other, waiting for one to say something to the other. We used to hold hands and hold each other. She would put her head on my chest or in my lap whenever I was watching television or just sitting. But when Kelly died, it's like we lost touch. We never get close to each other - we just sit there and stare at each other."

As relationships are examined today, communication is the single most important element that binds a couple together. Especially when it is effective. When it is not, the lack of communication becomes a repository for dissolution of most relationships.

Communication styles vary with each couple. Special ways of communicating effectively often develop with time and years together. Most couples say that trial-and-error methods guided them to their present stage of smooth sailing in communication.

Changes

Changes in communication patterns occur for a couple when they progress from the engagement and honeymoon periods to the marriage. Even topics of discussion change and become more focused on *we* and *our*, instead of *I* and *me*.

As the relationship grows, most couples let their guards down, so to speak, and share more of their inner selves with their mate. This process continues and escalates with longevity of the relationship.

At first, the couple's communication centers on each partner, gradually it centers more on the pair. The adding prospect of another family member often occurs once the couple feels safe in the longevity of their relationship.

Another significant change in the communication pattern occurs when the couple becomes pregnant. Discussions center on the growing family addition. The unborn child takes on an active role in the communication process when movement is noted. As the baby moves in response to touch, with increasing frequency, its position in the family is almost actualized.

The mother's abdomen grows, the father strokes and caresses her growing flesh. It is at this point that the baby is often called by name. Sometimes this playful activity takes place at the very outset of pregnancy. It is now that the dyad becomes a triad, as both parents try on their expected roles.

Couples often find themselves lost for words when attempting to talk following their baby's death. It is also very common for the mother and close relatives to question whether the father has actually grieved.

A noticeable change in the father's behavior toward his mate is confusing. This confusion occurs because most fathers are very demonstrative of their affection during pregnancy. Mothers usually do not question their mate's desire for the pregnancy. The reason this duplicity occurs is that visual evidence of pain is easily recognized and coded as such by society. This type of visual realization of emotions is also the case with most couples who experience their baby's death.

Mothers are given permission to grieve the moment death occurs. Everyone in a mother's environment realizes that she is bound to hurt after being pregnant for so long, even if the delivery ends prematurely. In most cases, she receives support for her frustration and anger. The father is at her side protecting her at this time.

Generally, fathers initially attend to the details of the baby's burial, take care of their wives, and handle day-to-day activities at home. When all of this is done, and the mother is progressing toward acceptance of the baby's death, usually most fathers start to grieve.

Unlike their partners, fathers often show signs of grieving in a different way. In society, it is deemed okay for women to cry. It is a natural response for anyone in this situation. Still, most fathers choose to cry away from their mates.

Conversations are strained. Unfortunately, most couples elect to avoid discussion of feelings. The fear of outbursts of rage and blaming accelerates. Many couples return to times of formal communication when their relationship was new. (Formality usually decreases as couples grow together.) During times of stress, if problems were present prior to the onset of the stressor, miscommunication often plagues the relationship.

There are three important aspects regarding the communication pattern between couples at this time:

(1) *avoidance* of the topic,

(2) invalidated *assumptions* about the feelings of their partner,

(3) perpetuation of *singling comments* with family members and friends.

Avoidance

To some people, the best way to prevent an argument is to avoid the topic at all costs. One or both partners are sometimes guilty of this offense. And an offense it is because the death of a baby actually occurred. The devastation both partners feel will not dissipate unless feelings are acknowledged. Both partners have to accept what is said by the other person. They must realize that no two people grieve the same way.

Personalities are different; therefore, expressions of emotions are consistent with a person's personality. No one can categorically exclaim, "I cried and the world saw my tears. Therefore, I grieved more than you."

Each partner should have reasonable expectations of their partner's manner of expressing their grief. Do not expect your partner's behavior to mirror your own. Your way is right for you. Allow your partner freedom of expression. Avoid barriers to communication by setting realistic expectations.

Assumptions

"I cry when I am alone, but my wife does not believe me. She wants me to cry in front of her. I cannot do that because I am a man. She says I just didn't give a damn about our baby."

Partners should avoid making assumptions about their mate's feelings. When one partner concludes that a certain level of grieving should occur and the other partner should display it in a specific way, the other person feels devalued and defends their feelings. Arguments follow when justifying behavior. Energy is expended fighting without a solution.

Assumptions regarding behavior without accurate validation are misguided. Conversations that lead to arguments will continue when one partner makes inaccurate assumptions. The partners become more distant and conversations are difficult, and the cycle of negative behavior continues. Separation is inevitable.

Healing cannot occur in the absence of positive communication. Positive arguing that focus on the immediate issue and ends with a resolution acts toward healing eventually. However, defending and supporting assumptions usually stagnates communication.

Singling Comments

"Joan, my heart just goes out to you. I know you hurt because of this. I'll think of you." (Gives the mother a hug and the father a smile.)

"Thank you, Ellen. You are so thoughtful."

Ben blurted out, when Ellen had left, "You acted like I wasn't even present."

"You didn't say anything. If you wanted to say something you should have."

"What would I say?" *Ellen, this hurts me, too. Give me a hug.* "No way, you could have included me."

This conversation was shared by a couple. The only difference is that on one occasion, a mother told the other person, "We are hurting, both of us are devastated." Those words meant a lot to her mate.

When well-wishers overlook the father, as in the former conversation, tension mounts. When one partner perceives that the other partner is allowing people to be insensitive, the couple continues to separate. It also serves as a point of discontent and a focal point for arguments.

Corrections are easy to make with family and friends when pronouncements of sympathy are given for the mother only. A simple statement would have corrected the singling comment: "Ellen, both of us are hurting."

Intimacy

Withdrawal from intimacy in a relationship seemed to be a mechanism used by some fathers to prevent another pregnancy. They feared being in the same situation too soon with another baby. However, abstinence as a coping mechanism was perceived as a way to control their relationship.

Some mothers believed their mates were involved in affairs. A need for time alone by fathers, months following the baby's death, was mislabeled as an attempt to be with another woman, especially when the frequency of sexual intercourse was decreased.

A small percentage of mothers yearned to become pregnant again soon after the death of their babies. However, fathers were not so eager. Read their comments.

"Suppose this happens again."

"There will be no more babies. I mean that."

"I'm sitting there and can't do anything."

"No, not now. It's just too early."

Couples soon become intimate strangers. The fear of another *failed* pregnancy dominates their approach to intimacy. Both partners must acknowledge their feelings and work toward healing. Their relationship has changed and is faced with new realities and multiple deaths--death of their anticipated family life and their expected family roles and functions.

Restoring Communication

Complete these exercises when you actually feel ready. Now is the time to become reacquainted. Start today to relive the events of your pregnancy. Working through these significant events will aid you as you attempt to grieve.

Preparation

First, free your environment of distractions. Turn off the ringers on your telephones. Do the same thing with your television, radio, washing machine, and other gadgets that make noise. Do not receive visitors. Schedule this activity when you have unhurried time. Begin when both of you consent willingly. If your partner tells you no, accept that response. Ask for a general time, but please, do not insist.

Activities

1. Think of your early pregnancy, the very moment when both of you felt the baby move. Describe your feelings for each other and for your baby. Take turns *hearing* each other. Do not interrupt!

2. Use *I* statements. Do not interpret what you hear. Ask for clarification.

3. As your discussion builds, emphasize events of the day, the very time you realized your pregnancy was in jeopardy. Share your feelings with your mate.

4. When your baby died, how did you feel?

5. What thoughts filled your mind and occupied your time?

6. Share with your mate what you wanted done for you that was not done.

Here is something else to try. When verbalizing your feelings is difficult, write your mate a letter. Allow your mate to read it in private before discussing the letter's contents. This activity is designed to enhance communication. Try talking about anything, laugh, cry, and share your feelings.

If either of you decide that your grief is still overwhelming, at that point--wait. The time will come soon enough for you to help each other toward healing. Maybe you still will not actually *see* your partner's tears, but know that they exist. Sometimes it is the female in the relationship who cannot allow anyone to see her tears.

Long-term communication for a couple is similar to learning a new dance. Both partners agree to try the new dance steps. As soon as a new step is perfected, it is time to learn a whole new approach. One partner is inhibited and the other partner must encourage them to try. With understanding, patience, and effort, the other partner loosens up. A new step is learned. Back and forth the partners go around the dance floor. Bumpy at first. After many steps together, repeating the steps over and over again, the new dance is learned.

Communication is the same way. Partners learn from each other. However, always remember one important point: It takes an open mind to keep communication flowing. Communication is a dance, back and forth, learning, forever changing, and finally, near-perfection. A key element is sharing. It is a gradual process. Any degree of disclosure works to enhance communication.

22

In Their Words

At the end of each interview, I asked fathers to provide insight for others who may have similar experiences in the future. Some fathers were eager to spare someone else the pain they have endured. The information included in this chapter is invaluable. Tables provide a brief list of thoughts, feelings, and needs expressed by fathers.

ADVISOR 1

If someone is experiencing this thing, I would say: Talk with your wife. Even though it is difficult, use *I* statements. Say, *I feel this way, I think this way*. That kind of communication works. It has been shown that a very high correlation exists between the death of infants and marital breakups.

That would be my main advice. *How* to do that is a whole other question, you see, but that is the main goal people should strive toward.

ADVISOR 2

My advice is for fathers to accept and understand their grief. No two people are alike. I can only speak for myself. I needed to be the strength of my family, although you know, that is kind of a fabricated position because I have never seen anything stronger than giving birth.

I cannot tell someone how to handle their grief because I don't try to be that typical male. I am not unemotional, but it is something that has been with me so long I have developed some type of understanding of what death is. I am sure that whatever happens in the future, I won't suffer more than I have in the past.

I would tell them don't be afraid to cry. I don't care where. In those situations, usually it comes at a hell of a

196

time. You never know when it is going to come.

ADVISOR 3

When our baby died, I could talk to my wife. It was much later though, but it was when I needed to. She is my best friend.

It helps to realign your priorities. We both have a strong faith in God. We don't wear it around on our shoulders, or we try not to. Our faith in God is what has seen us through. I can't imagine in today's hectic, fast-paced world how people can make it through tough times without strong faith.

I had a lot of anger. It helped to just yell at God. I later had guilt about that, too, but our minister thinks that it was healthy for us. Somewhere in the Bible, I think it says something about God understands.

Tell fathers not to feel guilty for feeling emotionless at the beginning, but try to get their emotions out at some time.

ADVISOR 4

If you can grieve on your own that is fine, but when you can't, find a relative or friend to talk with. If that doesn't work, get professional help. Everybody needs a shoulder to lean on.

I had big plans for Kamir. I think about him all the time. I really didn't know how to handle it. If I see an accident about to happen, I can avoid it. Other things in my life I can either avoid or control, but this was different. I couldn't handle it. I really thought about killing myself. I didn't do it because it would not have been a comfort for anybody. Fathers must think before they move. It [emotions] will come out eventually.

For people around another father, who might be going through this same thing, go to him, help him in some way. You know the man has got to be hurting; after all, he wanted the baby, too. Whatever you can do for him, do it, and try to do a little bit more. Just be a shoulder for him to lean on.

ADVISOR 5

I think it was Newton or someone like him who said, "One reaction causes another reaction." A man has got to do something about the grief at that point. If you stop it, just bury it, it is going to produce something you won't want. So if you don't handle your emotions, and you don't handle them constructively, it is going to drive you nuts.

If you know someone in this situation, it will be easier on them if you will verbalize your feelings and say something. It is hard to walk up to a stranger and say "I'm sorry" and expect them to believe it. But if I really knew the person, I would walk right up to him and try to console him. Both parents are going to need it, not just the mother.

Find a good listener. And people should be good listeners. These parents don't need anybody hovering over them; most of them are in total shock.

ADVISOR 6

When I felt myself getting tense, I would say to Kelly, "I'm not upset with you. I just need to be by myself for about an hour." Then I would put on my headphones and listen to music or something. About 80% of the time, I could get involved in my job and keep myself pretty busy. That is the key; keeping busy helped me. Of course, I would deal with the grief. Sometimes it just kind of overwhelmed me, and I couldn't control what happened.

So to other fathers, I would say to let it out [tears], even if you have to be by yourself. And another thing: Insist on a picture and even try to hold your baby no matter what conflict it causes. Let your baby know how much you wanted them to live.

ADVISOR 7

Parents, and especially the father, need to go through the whole works. It depends on the medical staff where you are. If they will let you hold the baby and be there the whole night, if that is when it occurs, hold and examine the baby.

If I could advise a father whose baby dies, I would say to him to find out all the details. What caused the problem? Make sure, that he cries when he feels the need. I cried when David died. Make the funeral arrangements and get someone to help you if you can.

Some support group meetings are really okay. It helped me just to hear other people talk about their feelings. You kind of compare what you think to what they are saying. It helps to know that you weren't feeling something wrong.

We took pictures in the labor room and when David was on the machines. We couldn't look at the pictures at first, but now they help us to know that David lived.

ADVISOR 8

There is one thing I can think of. Advice you give people often comes from mistakes you make. I got so emotionally overwrought, and so paranoid and so fearful of what was going to happen, that I separated myself from the baby.

It was like a paradox. On the one hand, I was so protective and concerned, and on the other hand, I was afraid of Cathy. We named her Cathy. Now that I have had a few months to think, I realize it was silly to think that her death may have been caused by them saying that she did not have a good chance. I thought that the more I got attached to her the more it is going to hurt.

So my biggest advice to a man who is going through this is don't get so immersed in the tragedy of it that you lose out on the time that you have with your baby. I made that mistake and there is no way I can ever rectify it.

When Cathy died, of all the bad things I was feeling, the guilt that was brought on, bore down on me more than anything else. I felt like I was a bad human being. So just treasure every minute you have with your baby.

ADVISOR 9

For fathers going through this now and in the future, I would tell them not to make any major changes in their lives. If you can, stick with your job. If you can, go in and talk with your boss or someone in authority and tell them the situation.

Before you do all of that, do some self-analysis. It's hard though. You'll get through it. You should take walks and take time off if you can. Realize that a major catastrophic event has occurred, and treat it as that. Don't try to stuff it under the rug or treat it as something else. Admit that it is affecting you. Be open and admit it. And seek out some help - you'll really need it.

It's going to take a few years to really deal with it. Just don't make any changes for a while.

ADVISOR 10

If they can ever get past the point of how to tell their wives what they feel, then their relationship won't get as touchy as ours did. When their wives ask them if they are okay, they should definitely open up. I don't care how hard it is. I haven't done it, but if there is any way they can force themselves, they should.

A question a wife can ask is: How angry are you? I found out today and it scared me. I never realized how much anger I could hold inside. That is probably the biggest thing for me, the anger and bitterness, I can feel it.

Before, I thought it was going away. But I could still bust somebody right now. Realize that you are going to be angry. So the best thing is to find a punching bag. Look at my fingers. See how purple they are? I hit the wall several times. It hurts; padded walls make a lot of sense.

They might want to join a group. See, I'm telling you things that I haven't done that maybe I should do. My cousin comes around and gets me to go places with him. That has helped me a lot.

ADVISOR 11

My advice is to let the grief come. Don't try to inhibit the feelings. Find someone to talk to. It would be good if your mate realizes that you are hurting, too. You just cannot be strong all the time for her.

It was good that when all of this happened, we were moved to another unit. At least we were away from all of the babies. Then again, in a way it was bad, because we were away from all of the nurses who knew about Katherine's needs.

ADVISOR 12

If I heard about a father today who was going through what we went through, I would go to him and tell him about our experience. I would pray with him and listen to what he has to say. I would just be there for him to lean on.

ADVISOR 13

I kind of lost my temper. That's what turned this thing around for me. I almost got fired for it. So on my job, they have a fantastic Employee Assistance program. So I got with the therapist and listened to some relaxation tapes. She said that I just needed to calm down and let the emotions out. That helped me. It will probably help someone else.

ADVISOR 14

First of all, I would tell him to forget about how he was treated at the hospital and by anybody else who didn't try to understand his feelings. It was business as usual for us. Like nothing ever happened. Our baby just died, and they seemed more concerned about regulations than about how we were feeling.

So he needs to put his anger aside about that and everything else, or he will never go on with his grief. Just remember that people are going to be the way they are no matter what.

He needs to ask for literature on grief so he can understand what is about to happen to him. Everybody has an angle, but he has to let somebody know how he is feeling, or he will never get help.

ADVISOR 15

My worst worry was how to explain to our three-year-old what had happened. He asked so many questions about his baby sister. I just knew that as soon as I saw him he would say, "Where is my sister?" So I called the support group leader who is our son's day care teacher. I asked if she would explain to Mike what had happened.

That was about three to four hours after I found out. I realized that I just didn't know what to say to him. Other fathers who might go through this same thing need to call on other people for help. Sometimes we have to force ourselves to do that.

I knew if I told him that Mama lost the baby he would

say, "I'll help you find her," or something like that.

Later on when I picked him up, we went to the hospital to see Regina. We were coming out and we passed a maternity window that was partially opened. I asked him if he wanted to see the babies. He said, "Which one is ours, Daddy?"

I said,"No son, ours is gone. Ours died, ours isn't here."

He said, "Oh. Where is ours, Daddy?" That just flat threw me for a loop. I didn't know how to respond. Then I went through it again. He was just too young to understand.

A man has got so much to think about. Just get some help. You have to force yourself to let other people in.

ADVISOR 16

Find somebody to talk to about it. If you feel like crying, and if you don't feel comfortable crying in front of somebody, go off somewhere and cry. But always talk to your spouse. Don't hold back. It's so easy for us to hold back or withdraw.

You just have to go through it. The pain and all are just part of the whole thing. But that pain is healing.

Some of the most frequently mentioned thoughts, feelings, and needs by fathers are listed in Tables 1, 2 and

3. They are separated into two periods: (1) early, on knowing that the baby is moribund (dying) or when the baby dies, and (2) later, after the occurrence of death or sometime after a burial.

The information included in all three tables provides a partial listing of descriptors provided by fathers. As you read them, realize that a father who seems detachment and unconcerned could actually be an advisor in this chapter.

Each of the three tables contains a section labeled EARLY. With these words extracted from conversations with fathers, it is obvious that they were baffled by their situation of death. Someone can use the information provided and volunteer to help a father with any confounding fact listed in the tables.

Table 1   THOUGHTS OF FATHERS

Early	Later
- what do I do next	-can't let it happen again
- did I screw up	- couldn't fix it
- this is hard	- can't believe it
- don't want to deal with questions about funeral arrangements	- to go by cemetery and let feelings out
- how to help mate	- for wife to get over grief
- be stabilizing force	- when will the hurt stop
- can't do anything about it	- people don't know me
	- that I didn't hold the baby
- not the way things are supposed to be	- part of me is gone that I can never replace
- I am to blame	- they are in heaven
- how am I going to handle this	- plans for the baby
	- about suing
	- trying to comprehend our friends
	- something happened to cause death

These thoughts occurred through out the
   couple's experience
- faith in God
- figure out what was going on
- friends and relatives don't understand

Table 2   FEELINGS OF FATHERS

Early	Later
- hit like a bolt	- difficult to survive
- ripped apart	- crashed
- floating around in void	- angry
- alone	- harder now
- falling apart	- guilty
- anger at God	- relief
- like something ripped your insides out	
- panic	
- loss of control, hurt, distraught	
- wanted to hit somebody	
- crying inside	
- sad and hurt inside	
- to break feelings loose	
- isolated and confused	
- devastated	
- in a daze	
- empty	
- like somebody put their hands in my body and took out my heart	
- stabbed to the quick	
- like someone beat the hell out of me	
These feelings occurred	
- frustrated	- scared
- numb	- frustrated and drained
-cheated and lonely	

Table 3	NEEDS OF FATHERS

Early	Later
- help with bureaucratic morass	- go by cemetery and let feelings out
- to cry and hug wife	- wife to get over grief
- a picture	- to stay busy
- to be alone	- a picture of my baby
- to be in a special room	- to keep my mind off of it
- to be with wife	- to write down what I felt
- to be in on decisions	
- to name baby	

- time to make decisions re: funeral arrangements
- to ask questions and get answers
- nurses to talk to me more about what is going on

Needs occurred throughout the grief experience:

- someone to talk to	-to get away
- how to handle things	-time off from work

- someone to ask how I am doing
- something to ease the hurt
- someone to care about me
- for wife to see our baby
- how to talk to a wife
- a little peace of mind
- a shoulder to lean on, support from friends
- to be recognized as a human being
- wives to hold, hug, and take care of me, too
- for someone to say everything will be okay
- to be braced for what people would say

23

Are You Guilty?

Hoof-and-mouth disease is a common phenomenon that transcends all cultures and languages. The term simply requires translation. It happens all over the world. Without thinking, sometimes the wrong words just jump out of our mouths. When it happens, it's too late to retrieve ill-spoken words. Try as you might to patch up what you have done, already your words have harmed someone.

I admire people who always know the right thing to say on every occasion. But that is not the way of the world.

Somewhere, someone out there is hurting someone's feelings right now without knowing it.

Times of grief are not exceptions. Just what do you say? And what do you do?

This chapter includes an assessment of well-intentioned statements by sympathizers. With time, parents realized that these statements did more harm to them than good. When you simply cannot think of one good thing to say, remember, it is better to say nothing. Give the person a hug and keep going. If you feel compelled to comfort with words of wisdom, read this chapter carefully. Maybe the information here will prevent you from opening mouth and inserting your foot.

1. *You are young. You can have more children.*

What about *this* child? Each baby conceived brings a unique experience for the couple. The couple will probably have more children, but this statement makes it seem as though it is okay for a couple to suppress feelings for their baby. If something happens, just have another one. It is not that simple.

2. *It's been [some arbitrary length of time]. You should be over that now.*

Another inappropriate statement. The baby should be called by name or referred to as *Baby* and not *it* or *that*. Even though "it" is appropriate when speaking of a baby.

212

At the time of death, parents may view the speaker as being insensitive.

There is no hard and fast rule for when grief should subside. Pathological grief is one thing, but normal grief can last a lifetime.

When a neighbor's daughter goes to the prom, a father may have thoughts of his child participating in the prom if she had lived. Maybe a tear is shed in private.

3. *It's not like she was ever alive.*

This statement baffles me. Yet people think they are sharing in a person's grief by making this kind of insensitive comment. We could debate for decades the issue of when the onset of life occurs, again, that is not the issue here. Be tactful, consider miscarriages as a very private part of a couple's life. Do not speak of the ended pregnancy as though it were nothing.

4. *Well, it was for the best. He might have been deformed.*

How do you know this? Maybe it *was* for the best; however, this statement seems self-serving. If you have nothing to say, do that: say nothing. Tell the couple that you wish you knew just the right thing to say to help them get through their grief. Admit that you don't, hug them, and leave.

5. *How is Sally? Tell her I am thinking about her.*

Unless Sally is a single woman who was artificially inseminated, to make this kind of statement without also acknowledging the father's pain is inappropriate. The man you give this message to has feelings. It is not as though Sally became pregnant alone. The father also loved the baby or child that died.

If you are uncomfortable talking to a man about how he feels, give him a hug. Tell him that you will think of him, pray for him, etc. Remember, in the dreams of most fathers, they have already planned college for their child. The memories will never go away.

6. *You must be strong for [your wife].*

Why? Even if he decides to do just that, keep this kind of comment to yourself. He is the father. He hurts, too. Tell him, "I may not know what to say, but I am a great listener. Maybe we can go out and shoot a game of pool, get a beer, or just go for a ride." When time passes without a phone call from him, get on the phone and offer your time. Now is a perfect time to make an unannounced visit. This is your friendship. Judge what is best for your friend who needs a shoulder to lean on.

7. *I'll call you sometime. (The friend never does.)*

Whatever you do, do not forget to circle a date to call on your calendar. Plan to spend time with the father doing exactly what you did before, or what he wants. Of course, this will take time. Allow time in your schedule to hear your friend recount the events that led to the death of his baby and the redirection of his life. If you are a friend, be a friend now.

8. *Call me if you need me.*

Do not allow your mouth to utter these words insincerely. If you absolutely want to help a couple get through their grief, try driving the father somewhere after he learns that his baby is dead. Call to ask if he has eaten. See if he needs someone to help with a decision. If the mother is still hospitalized, does she need toilet items, a gown, a hug? If you are sincere, be available.

9. *I didn't see you cry; so, did you grieve? Or: You are handling everything just fine.*

Realize that some people cry in private. Absence of tears in your presence is not a measure of the grief that is felt. You cannot judge how a person feels strictly by nonverbal behavior or physical cues. Assume that the grief is there.

10. *I know how you feel.*

You do not! This statement brings comfort to no one. You cannot possibly know how the person feels, especially if you have not experienced the death of a child. This is not your time to shine. So stop a minute and realize the depth of the person's situation.

11. *At least you have another child.*

Each baby's life is unique. The couple may in fact have another baby, or they may have another child at home. But the death of this baby has just occurred. The birth, *anticipated life* and death of this child deserve recognition.

12. *You can always have another child.*

A couple cannot think of having another child until they have healed and grieved for the baby who has just died. This statement is insulting, cavalier, and not needed at this time.

13. *Let's not talk about that right now.*

When *will* you allow time for the person to air their feelings? *Never* is probably the response, because the next time the subject comes up, the father may not be as open or willing to have you as a confidant.

This statement allows you to protect yourself when you do not have anything to say. I have been told that the speaker of these words is trying to keep the person's mind off the death. Believe me, someone actually thought they had helped the father. *Think again!* Talking about the event allows the person to recount positive acts with their baby, and grieving can begin.

14. *Get on with your life.*

You cannot tell another person when to stop grieving. However, it is possible to identify that a person is having difficulty with their grief. Offer assistance. Make suggestions to the father or couple for counseling. Remember, the deceased baby was part of their future. For approximately nine months the couple had placed their baby in their lives and in their future. They have to grieve the dreams that will not occur before they can move on.

15. *I heard that his brain was normal and he had so many other deformities, it's just best this way. He never could have made it in this society.*

So quick to judge. Babies are born each and every day with deformities that do not alter their ability to think and to love. Most adapt to life and do well. It is not our place to judge. To avoid this major insult, make no mention of rumors regarding the child's physical or mental status. If the couple wants to share that information, they will.

16. *You must be careful when you are pregnant.*

Never use words that suggest the couple may have initiated their baby's death. Keep your unfounded suspicions to yourself. All the caution in the world cannot prevent nature's course from occurring.

I am certain there are other equally insensitive statements. Remember, before you open your mouth to console a couple or even a relative put yourself in the other person's place. Just maybe, the act of doing so will aid you as you try to bring comfort.

If you know of nothing to do or say, do and say exactly that, nothing. Offer a hug, be a listener, and check on the couple in the difficult weeks and months to come.

24

It's My Turn

It is amazing to me that, in spite of all the technological innovations in society today, about as much is understood regarding fathers and their feelings as was understood fifty years ago. The knowledge hierarchy *seems* devoid of information that could simplify life for fathers.

However, this is far from the truth. A few very reputable authors have written palatable summaries that lie dormant on dusty library shelves. Volumes are filled with information compiled from studies that hint and expound on fathering and family life. Somehow this array of information has not found its way into the public domain for consumption in everyday life.

Still, knowledge about mothers far exceeds that about fathers. In the past, most researchers were men. They studied women. This practice occurred because there was a consensus among male researchers that men did not have the emotional imbalances that women certainly must have. So, when most research was conducted, women were subjects.

Another possible rationale for the imbalance in information is society's transcultural labeling of men as being "strong" and "able to control their emotions." Women are considered to be the weaker gender. There also is an unstated axiom in society that *if a person can control emotions, the emotion must not be of great consequence for them.*

In decades past, the significance of fathers in the family system paralleled societal changes. During the 1950's, John Bowlby wrote that fathers in the '50s were of no great value to the child, except in economic and emotional support. Other philosophers and theorists disseminated equally insipid statements. Fortunately, society's myopic view is forging toward a panoramic picture of family life that includes the behavior of fathers and their emotional life.

Eric Fromm, noted psychoanalyst, believed that culture helps to shape the personality. In his writing he emphasized the importance of the father to a child. He wrote that fathers inspire children to self-criticism and achievement in the external world. Critics would probably explain this statement as an outcome of mothers in the '50s and '60s being occupied with full-time employment as homemakers.

Fromm is not alone. Other experts have written about the necessity of fathers in family systems. However, society seems to neglect fathers and represent them as a point for mockery. What is required for society to perceive fathers as essential and exemplary parents? How much more and how much longer must fatherhood require examination?

And, do fathers really understand the impact of their involvement in their child's life? Do they know what they do? Or are they listening to the baseless dialogues by misinformed authorities who subvert the fabric of family roles?

In that regard, how many summaries of studies on fathers and their grief experiences must permeate the media before society believes that a man also grieves when his baby dies? Points presented in this book also apply to fathers when their child suffers, when their child is deeply troubled, or when their child's life takes a path that is not productive to society.

When I remember the fathers I have interviewed, I wish that I could thank each one again for the wealth of information they provided that made this book possible. Their collective stories shed light on a sensitive topic that has profound meaning.

Almost every father mentioned his surprise when he discovered the cathartic effect of talk. In some cases, I recommended additional counseling. Some fathers considered these sessions to be therapeutic. At the end of each interview, I observed that the father's face and body were more relaxed. Each seemed to have a heightened awareness of his experience.

When fathers were joined by their mates for the interviews, during and following debriefing I observed as they took in a new realization of their husband's feelings. All of the wives admitted to being unaware of the depth of pain their mates had shared at the time.

All facts in this book were extracted from interviews. Facts are listed that affect fathers, mates, relatives, friends, social support groups, hospital personnel, employers, and clergymen. Follow these points to enhance communication with a spouse, friend, or anyone who grieves the death of a child, or during any crisis:

General Points of Interest:

1. Comments made by fathers regarding what they felt, thought, and needed did not differ among races, ages, and cultures of fathers. Gender differences are more significant when tragedy occurs.

2. All fathers were able to describe their initial grief reactions in the hospital or wherever the death occurred.

3. A majority spoke of wanting to be alone for a while. Fathers whose budgets allowed for such a necessity actually took a vacation; others did not.

4. Most fathers had no one to talk to initially because their wives were recovering from the effects of anesthesia or they were in pain. Other fathers talked to no one.

5. A majority of fathers said they wanted to tell their mates how they felt but could not find words to express their feelings.

6. Fathers said that their mates should have known how they felt, because they had wanted the pregnancy from the beginning.

7. All fathers in the study simply wanted respect for their anticipated fathering role; none had a need to make anyone uncomfortable with their tears.

Tips For Fathers

1. Write down how you feel. Don't worry about your ability to write just scribble your thoughts on paper. Write the first thing that comes to mind. Start with the day of delivery and allow your thoughts to flow to your paper.

2. If you are a visual learner, ask for pamphlets. If the hospital has nothing to offer, call a local support group or visit your local library. If all else fails, and maybe it should be the first thing you do, get in contact with me through "Fathers Talk" P.O. Box 6427, Columbus, GA 31907. See

Appendix D for more information.

3. Try a support group to resolve your feelings. If this intervention is not for you, call a counselor. Look in the yellow pages or call Ask-A-Nurse at your local hospital.

4. Plan a day of fishing, drive to the cemetery where your baby is buried, go for a long drive, jog in the country, go bowling, find a gym, or just sit on the beach. Do whatever you normally do to solve problems. However, get involved with constructive activities.

Tips For Mates

1. Always consider your mate's needs. If he says "I'm okay," give him a loving hug. Most men do not know how to ask for tenderness during times that render them less than the all-controlling-male.

2. Realize that expressions of his emotions will be similar to other situations in your lives. An unexpressive man is not going to become a great orator or interpreter of his emotions during a crisis.

3. Every human has feelings, thoughts, and needs during every situation. Some people are able to voice their needs immediately; others find it difficult. Some people even consider divulging their inner sanctum as an imposition. Get to know your mate during a crisis. *Assume nothing*.

4. Also, ask for clarification when you talk with your mate. But do not question or criticize him for expressing

how he feels in a communication pattern and manner that is different to you. He is not alone. When you think about it, feeling as though your "heart has been ripped out" is descriptive for pain a father feels.

Hospital Personnel

1. Redevelop your protocol for parents when a baby dies.

2. Save all garments worn by the baby for at least one month, even if initially the parents say they do not want them. Call *all parents* after one month to see how they are doing. Ask about the clothes. Discard them at this time if the parents still do not want them.

Storage of these tiny items is a minor inconvenience for a hospital that may have problems with space. To save a couple a lifetime of regret is worth every inch of shelf-space the small items occupy.

3. Pictures are an absolute necessity, regardless of the hospital's size. If funding is not available, make connections with a community group that can support your efforts to become more parent-oriented. A picture taken with an instamatic camera verifies that a couple's baby existed. The photo will be treasured for years to come, even though at the time of death the parents' first response maybe that they do not want a picture.

4. Take time to allow each parent to hold their baby. If this is not possible, at least allow the parents to place the

baby in their hands. Even a moribund baby connected to a ventilator can be held on the isolette table. *Find a way!* Save parents years of regret.

Allow parents to participate in taking care of their baby's needs, even if death is inevitable. Think of the planning entailed when you allow parents to care for a normal baby. I am aware that the two events are worlds apart. Devote time to allow parent participation when death is near for their baby. When a parent participates in the activities surrounding the death of their baby, the unfinished business of that death does not linger quite as long.

5. Never assume that a support group is the only effective method for grief resolution. Purchase a copy of *a cassette series and booklet, Fathers Cry, Too--A Grief Resolution Program* (available January 1996 from Family Projects Publishers). Fathers use driving time to sort through their problems. Put that time to use for them because not every father will participate in a support group. Provide the cassette tape program for their use, or inform them of its availability.

6. Discourage *singling comments* by revising your grief education programs for personnel (Chapter 21). A couple's marital status should not alter the degree of consultation that is offered. Remember, on this occasion two people are joined by the death of their baby. Discourage comments that make parents feel isolated and eventually affect how they grieve.

7. Consider all activities during the resuscitation of a baby. When the action of resuscitation is over, go immediately to the father. Bring him into the area, if possible. Do not leave him in the hallway wondering what is going on behind closed doors.

8. Provide parents with written information. This procedure may seem insensitive to some hospital personnel; however, parents want information especially fathers. If you provide an Ask-A-Nurse service, include a phone number in the discharge package you give parents. Request that assigned nurses call parents a week or longer after the baby's death. If this is not possible, appoint a nursery nurse to call them.

9. Assess your actions and attitudes regarding the death of a baby, child, and adult. Do not develop coping mechanisms to handle the myriad of critically ill and moribund patients by forgetting that lives are affected by death. Fathers, as parents, need considerations similar to those given mothers when a baby dies.

Relatives, Friends, and Acquaintances

1. Reread Chapter 23.

2. Realize that your nonjudgmental support is essential at this time. There is no time limit on grief. (Leave it to the professionals to diagnose problem behavior as pathological.)

If you are sincere about wanting to help, allocate time to complete some of the following activities while the baby is hospitalized or when the baby dies.

a. Voice a genuine desire to help. Mention that you may not know the appropriate thing to say, but you will listen.

b. Contact a clergyman if agreed.

c. If the baby is hospitalized, visit or contact the nursery.

d. Be a friend, regardless of any angry words that may be voiced by either parent. A friend can tolerate the brunt of misguided words during times of high anxiety.

e. Contact friends and relatives and inform them of the situation.

f. Respond to phone calls from concerned callers.

g. Record the names of people who visit, send flowers, etc.

h. Provide transportation for the father, and go with him when the mother is discharged from the hospital

i. Arrange for yard service or do it yourself, and remember to water all plants.

j. Pay bills or simply separate the mail.

k. Assist with funeral arrangements.

l. Contact the nursery and ask for a picture of the baby or item of clothing.

m. Create a baby book. Save it for the parents, and give it to them later.

n. Make sure the father has a clean suit and other clean clothes.

o. Check to see if the mother needs items of clothing while in the hospital.

p. Put the garbage out for pick-up.

q. See if the refrigerator needs cleaning, emptying, or restocking.

r. Check on pets.

s. Offer your home to out-of-town guests that you may or may not have met.

t. If the couple has other children, offer to care for them for awhile, or talk with them about their sibling.

u. Listen to both parents.

v. Listen to the mother.

w. Listen to the father.

x. Listen to the father.

y. Listen to the father.

z. Acknowledge your feelings.

Places of Worship and Community Support Groups

1. Support groups, do not leave the provision of support to chance. Establish bylaws or other measures which ensure that concerned consultation is provided. Establish guidelines for attending to the needs of both parents.

2. Contact various forms of media and announce meeting information: dates, times, location. (These announcements are free for nonprofit organizations.)

3. Ministers, find a source of education on this topic. Find and offer literature to the parents when you visit them.

4. Ministers should prepare counsel for both parents. During visitation, speak to both parents, do not isolate them further by referring to the needs of the mother.

5. When ministers were asked about their approach to couples when a baby dies, a majority gave lengthy explanations of the mother's needs, but most clergymen were without adequate information for fathers. A large percentage had not thought of the father as being in need at that time. Some of them even said, "Oh no, fathers are usually okay. They are in control."

Whenever possible, help fathers relive events leading to the end of pregnancy. Fathers consistently mentioned thinking about activities they might have changed and their part in causing the baby's death. Help fathers to understand that they may have solutions to some of life's pressing problems, but determining and sustaining life is out of their hands.

Employers

1. Male employees should receive the same treatment afforded female employees when the death of a baby occurs. If a card is sent to a female employee, do the same for a male. If donations are collected, flowers are delivered, or extended sick time is offered, do the same for male

employees.

2. On the job, a man is less likely to show signs of grieving. Look for signs of exhaustion as your employee tries to sublimate his feelings through work.

Look for signs of unusual behavior following the baby's death. Was punctuality a problem before? Was your employee more tolerant of his co-workers before? If he now comes to work disheveled, or late, or has a temper, these are probable signs of an attempt to mask his feelings. Be aware of his need to grieve and have time away from his job without worrying about his employment status.

3. Design a program of stress reduction or simply suggest that he take a few days off. Designate someone to call and see how he is doing.

For Fathers--Initiating the Grief Process

1. *Acknowledge your role as your baby's father for a relationship that might have been.*

Only you know about plans you had for your child's life. Acknowledge that those dreams are gone for you and this child. Think about the time you did have together, even though it was before your baby's birth. Stroking your mate's stomach in response to your baby's kick was actually playtime. Treasure those moments.

2. *Acknowledge what is inside your mind and your heart.*

Take time to think about where you are right now and

what has transpired. Do not ignore that a tragedy has occurred and that you are devastated by the events.

3. *Associate your behavior with your feelings.*

Has your behavior changed suddenly? How? Why? Concentrate on your feelings. Being alone in a room so you can write down your thoughts might help. Look for definite answers that explain your behavior.

Changed behaviors are usually manifestations of frustrating emotions. Acknowledge your feelings. *But don't ever apologize for hurting.*

4. *Share your feelings with at least one other person.*

Talking clears the mind and heart. Hopefully the person you select to talk with is the baby's mother. If not, start with someone and talk with your mate later. Don't assume that she knows how you feel simply because of the length and depth of your relationship.

5. *You decide when it is time to move on, when it is bearable to think and talk about the relationship that will not exist with your baby.*

What is right for someone else is not necessarily right for you. You decide. You will acknowledge when that time occurs.

Comments

One fact is clear from the study: Fathers had much in common in the way they handled their grief. Race, ethnicity, religiosity, socioeconomic status, and geographic location did not affect the way they grieved or were perceived by family members and friends. However, economic differences did affect the way fathers handled their grief.

Fathers who could afford to get away did so without hesitation after their baby's death. Fathers whose budgets would not withstand the expense of a trip could only voice a desire to get away for awhile.

Most fathers mentioned that they were able to think about what had happened in their lives while commuting to and from work. Driving alone offered the greatest degree of solace, while going to the cemetery to "let it all out" was mentioned as the most long-term therapeutic activity.

The gender of the baby had no bearing on the severity of the experience for fathers, nor did length of pregnancy. Nevertheless, most fathers perceived their baby as being part of their families once they had felt its movement.

All fathers mentioned having thought about long-term plans for their unborn child. It was at that point that most babies were given affectionate names. Some fathers mentioned how they had planned to encourage education, and others talked about dating ages they had foreseen for their daughters.

Some fathers endured circumstances that compounded their difficult experience. Many of them mentioned unusually strained employment relations, being fired just before the baby's death, financial difficulties, and family disputes.

When self-counsel did not work, some fathers requested overtime. Many fathers volunteered for additional assignments at work and reported working longer hours than ever to prevent thoughts of their baby from surfacing. Others used smoking, drinking, or drugs to numb feelings about their dead baby.

For Fathers

There are many impediments to a father's expression of grief. Most of them center around gender and role identity: being strong, self-sufficient, the family protector, problem-solver/predictor, and controller.

Your memories will live with you forever, but no one can begin to know the extent of your pain. Start now to allow at least one person to share what is in your heart.

Do whatever it takes to turn your nightmare into a bearable daydream. I hope this book has been of some consolation. It is written with everyone in mind, so others may have a sense of what it is like to grieve unacknowledged and be able to share in and support your process.

25

Directions for Fathers

W hat is on the horizon for fathers? For the '90s, and especially in the twenty-first century, it is inevitable that changes will occur for fathers, just as shifts in thinking will ensue for society. Don't get your hopes up though: Men are not slated to start sharing their feelings on demand in the near future.

Radical changes in behavior for fathers as a group are not imminent. But subtle changes will occur that support acknowledgment of their emotional role and function within a family system. Remember that individual differences exist. Many fathers do not have a problem sharing their feelings. According to Nancy Gibbs in an article in *Time Magazine*, society is not quite ready to accept men's fears...or their sadness. Men are preferred as protectors and that role is lost if their emotional life is acknowledged.

When I drop off and pick up my daughter from day care, it is apparent that times are changing. Last week I counted seven fathers with their children as I drove away.

Big deal, you say. These fathers were probably on their way to work, so they dropped their child off on the way. Maybe and maybe not.

These fathers had other children with them who weren't yet walking. One had a baby in a front carrier who could not have been three months old. Now *that* is a dramatic change from days gone by!

Soon the media will catch up and redefine "normal" behavior for fathers. Research exists; however, the number of studies conducted must increase and the results be disseminated to the public.

Good behavior rarely makes the news, and when it does the public pays little attention to it. Consistent behavior that is descriptive of a father's multi-faceted role should be documented for fathers who are without role models.

The future holds promise for fathers as functioning members of family systems. Paternal leave is being discussed and offered in some circles. On October 24, 1993,

Knight-Ridder newspapers carried a story on male leave featuring two fathers who decided to take leave to spend more time with their children. Both men were surprised by the ease with which their employer honored their requests. However, both still felt a need to prove their abilities when they returned to work.

The business community has not changed to the extent that paternal leave is without stigma. We still operate in an arena where such a person's devotion to getting the job done is questioned by many, when seemingly unstructured, meaningless, lackluster time is put first.

Men's journals on mental and physical health and contemporary issues are prolific. There was a time when the only magazines designed for men were sports topics, pornographic, or how-to manuals for the at-home-repairman.

The same evolution has occurred in the book industry. Books on men's health issues are making their entry into the market and receiving rave reviews. According to the fathers interviewed, men want answers to puzzling topics. They seek information on masculinity, fatherhood, relationships, spirituality, communication, sexuality, and marriage.

In the future, more and more manufacturers and business owners will produce products and services that cater to single fathers and fathers traveling with small children. Most diaper bags and other baby products are frilly and brightly colored. Some are even cumbersome for the most agile female. Soon, manufacturers will realize the potential market that exists among the male population for less obtrusive items.

Likewise, more public agencies and businesses will install diaper tables in men's restrooms. Can you imagine a father trying to change a baby's diaper in a typical male restroom? No changing table! Even fathers with spouses occasionally take their children on outings without their mates.

In this decade, men and fathers will examine their grief experiences. They will continue to deal with them in a way that is familiar to them. However, they will also begin to consider outside input to their internal turmoil. They want the curtain to drop regarding myths that separate the genders during grief. However, some critical behaviors and habits are sacred. Maybe the next decade will see the results of changes which are initiated now.

Fathers who are active members of their family systems are vital to the success of their children. Many single mothers do a fantastic job of raising their child alone. However, in a household where the father is as responsible for his family as the mother, children tend to excel.

When I consider my four brothers, I think of what a blessing they received having our Dad as a father. All of my brothers can cook, and two of them can make a chef think twice before he serves a meal. I remember my father saying, "You have to learn everything there is to know about running a household. You always need to do your share at home. You'll need to be independent, especially when your wife gets pregnant and goes to the hospital to have a baby. And you won't need to depend on anybody for anything, because you'll know how to run your own household. Then you can get help because you need it, and not because you just don't know where to start."

Today, more than ever, I appreciate my father for teaching me, (along with my brothers) about household repairs. I'm sure my brothers appreciate knowing how to cook and sew, in addition to all the traditional male activities. In the future, more boys will receive the same kind of upbringing. It only serves to make a person more flexible.

I cannot end this section without mentioning fathers as single parents. On December 14, 1992, an article appeared in *Newsweek* titled, "It's Not Like Mr. Mom." The article was compiled by five authors. It reported that the number of single fathers was almost 15% in 1991, or 1.2 million households. According to the authors, one benefit of this switch, is that non-custodial mothers stay in contact with their children more than non-custodial fathers.

My youngest brother is in the Air Force. He is raising his three children as a single father. To look at their home you cannot tell that a woman is not present. He takes time with his children. They know him as a father and a friend.

As the number of men who head single households increases, society will make way for this new genre of fathers. Information which perpetuates old stereotypes about their roles will require revision in literature published for them.

As emphasis is placed on a return to family values, our opportunity is here. We can begin this revival by giving fathers the support they need to fulfill their role, and to grieve when necessary.

Epilogue:

The Future Is Brighter

I s this the end of the discussion on fathers' grief? No, not a chance.

I believe it is a beginning, as fathers everywhere realize that others in a similar situation feel the same as they do. The information presented here has been mentioned by other authors throughout the scientific community for years. Somehow the word has not reached massive numbers of people.

Looking over the events of the past two decades, it seems ironic that society still has a problem realizing that fathers are human beings. Yet we wonder about their health problems and longevity.

As mentioned at the beginning of this book, the issue dealt with herein concerns the man who takes his present and future role as a father seriously. It is not about other problems that plague men and women as we attempt to coexist.

Now, at the end of our dialog, it is important for the reader to realize that fathers cry just like anyone else. Their tears may not be as evident as mothers' tears, but they do occur.

If you are genuinely concerned about a father and his feelings - or a man in any setting who grieves - take what he tells you about his turmoil at face value. There is nothing more to know or be gained by judging what you have not experienced.

In some instances, men are slow to change. Men and women simply show their emotions differently. Even though tears are not apparent, it does not mean that the father is devoid of emotions during a crisis situation. What it does mean is that society has set an ominous paradox for parents, with entrenched rules that allow mothers to show their emotions through tears, while fathers are to generally handle emotions in a way they interpret as gender appropriate behavior.

In time, changes will occur. But for now, accept fathers as they are - and for many - that is with hidden emotions.

Remember to encourage expression of feelings. Above all else, listen.

PART VII: APPENDICES

Appendix A

Figure 1. Comparison of Grief Stage Theorists

Theorists Termination	# of Stages	Physical	Psychological	Social Spiritual	Final
Kubler-Ross	4-5	denial and shock	rage and anger	bargaining	acceptance
Lindemann	4	shock and disbelief	acute dysphoria	social withdrawal	resolution
Bowlby	4	numbness and shock	pining and yearning	disorganization	reorganization
Parkes	4	preoccupation	hostility	appeal for help and support	reorganization
Engel	3	shock and denial	developing awareness	---	resolution
Lamers	4	protest	despair	detachment	resolution
EVENT: permanent loss of significance or separation		Shock	Anger	Rationalization	Resolution
behavioral indicators		b.i.	b.i.	b.i.	b.i.

247

Appendix B

References and Related Literature

Bem, S. L. (1974). The measurement of psychological androgyny. *The Journal of Consulting and Clinical Psychology, 42,* 155-162.

Bem, S. L. (1981). *Bem-sex role inventory.* Palo Alto: Consulting Psychologists Press, Inc.

Canfield, J. & Hansen, M. (1993). *Chicken soup for the soul.* Dearfield Beach, FL: Health Communi., Inc.

Cole, D. (1992). *After great pain: A new life emerges.* New York: Summit Books.

Cornils, S.P. (1990). *The mourning after: How to manage grief wisely.* Saratoga, CA: R & E Publishers.

Coxe, P. (1994). *Letting go and finding peace.* Naperville, IL: Sourcebooks, Inc.

Creel, H. G. (1972). *Chinese thought from Confucius to Mao Tse-tung.* Chicago: The University of Chicago Press.

Davies, P. (1988). *Grief: Climb toward understanding.* New York: A Lyle Stuart Book.

DePaulo, J. R. & Ablow, K. R. (1989). *How to cope with depression.* New York: A Fawcett Crest Book.

DiGiulio, R. (1993). *After loss.* Waco: WRS Pub. Co.

Easwaran, E. (1992). *Your life is your message.* Tomales, CA: Nilgiri Press.

Epstein, A. (1993). *How to be happier day-by-day.* New York: Penguin Books.

Fromm, E. (1956). *The art of loving*. New York: Bantam Books.

Gay, P. (1989). *The Freud reader*. New York: W. W. Norton & Co.

Gibbs, N. R. (1993). Bringing up father. *Time, 141*(26), 52-61.

Goldberg, H. (1986). The hazards of being male. *Men's Health, 1*(1), 69-72.

Grier, R. (1986). *Rosey: An autobiography, the gentle giant.* Tulsa, OK: Honor, a Div of Harrison House.

Kimbrell, A. (1991). A time for men to pull together. U*nte Reader, 45,* 66-74.

Kubler-Ross, E. (1969). *On death and dying*. New York: MacMillan Publishers.

Laing, R. D. (1967). *The politics of experience*. New York: Pantheon Books.

Lord, J. (1990). *No time for goodbyes*. Ventura, CA: Pathfinder Publishers.

Mead, M., & Newton, N. (1967). Cultural patterning of perinatal behavior. In S. Richard & A. Guttmacher (Eds.), *Childbearing: Its social and psychological aspects* (pp. 104-108). Baltimore: The Williams & Wilkins Co.

Miller, J. (1978). *The healing power of grief.* New York: Seabury Press.

Parkes, C. M. (1972). *Bereavement: Studies of grief in adult life*. London: Tavistock.

Parkes, C. M., & Weiss, R. S. (1983). *Recovery from bereavement. New York: Basic Books, Inc.*

Rando, T. (1986). *Loss and anticipatory grief.* Lexington, Mass: Lexington Books.

Seligmann, J., Rosenberg, D., Wright, P., Hannan, D. &
Annin, P. (1992). It's not like Mr. Mom. *Newsweek*,
120(24).
Ullian, D. Z. (1976). The development of conceptions of
masculinity and femininity. In B. Lloyd & J. Archer
(Eds.), *Exploring sex differences.* (pp.25-47). New
York: Academic Press.

Appendix C

Support Groups

Compassionate Friends

A self-help organization offering friendship and understanding to bereaved parents. The organization's purposes are to promote and aid parents in the positive resolution of grief experienced when a child dies, and to foster physical and emotional health of bereaved parents and siblings.

There are over 630 chapters nationally. For information regarding a chapter near you contact the national office:

(708) 990-0010

P. O. Box 3696

Oak Brook, IL 60522.

National Sudden Infant Death Syndrome Foundation (SIDS)

Provides information and support to parents who have lost a baby through SIDS. Maintains current data on SIDS

2 Metro Plaza, Suite 205

8240 Professional Place

Landover, MD 20785

(301) 459-3388

International Childbirth Education Association (ICEA)
Provides information about local childbirth classes and support groups, newsletter and literature.
P. O. Box 20048
Minneapolis, MN 55420
(612) 854-8660

National Association for Down's Syndrome (NADS)
Provides information about Down's Syndrome to families, professionals, and community groups.
290 W. Fullerton Avenue
Addison, IL 60101
(312) 543-6060

Share
St Elizabeth's Hospital
211 S. Third Street
Belleville, IL 62222
(618) 234-2415

Candlelighters Childhood Cancer Foundation
2025 Eye St., NW
Suite 1011
Washington, D.C. 20006

The amount of information included for each group is not an indication of its merit. At press time, the author obtained information for groups with summaries.

Appendix D

Men's magazines and newsletters

Fathers Talk
Family Projects
    Publishers
3009 Hamilton Road
P. O. Box 6427
Columbus, GA 31907
(Newsletter printed six times per year with feature topics; letters from fathers welcomed and featured.)

Dad Magazine
Carol Lippert
65 Brookside Drive
Sparta, NJ 07871-2912

Men's Health
Michael Lafavore
Editorial Offices
Emmaus, PA 18098

Men Only
Nevile Player
2 Archer St
London Wiv7he,
Gr.BRITIAN

Exercise For Men
Chen Nam Low
350 5th Ave, #6204
New York, NY 10118-0110

GQ Magazine
Johnson Publishing Co.
820 S. Michigan Ave.
Chicago, IL 60605

Healthy Man
Jay Rosenfield
460 W. 34th St
Washington, DC 20005

Men's Journal
John Rasmus
1290 Ave of the Americas
New York, NY 10104-0298

Men's Life
Phyllis Halliday, Books
2 Park Ave, #4
New York, NY 10016-5601

Index

Write The Author

Do you have an interesting story to tell about your father? Now that you are older, do you realize there were lessons in surviving life that your father taught you? Do you think other people can benefit from your fathers teachings? If so, take time to write your story, 10-25 double spaced typed pages. Maybe your story will appear in print along with many others as a book on fathers. If you are interested, write to the address below. Details will follow in the mail.

> FAMILY PROJECTS PUBLISHERS
> 3009 Hamilton Road
> P. O. Box 6427
> Columbus, Georgia 31907
> ATTN: Stories on Fathers

Speaking Engagements

Dr. Turner is available to speak to your group or for consultation. She has addressed lay and professional groups all over the United States and other countries. Audiences enjoy her rare brand of humor and method of presentation. She summarizes the topic of fathers and their grief experience in a manner that leaves everyone informed and renewed. Contact Molley Nielsen to arrange an engagement with Dr. Turner at 706/687-4296.